PARENTING
TO BUILD CHARACTER
IN YOUR TEEN

Also from the Boys Town Press

Common Sense Parenting®
Common Sense Parenting of Toddlers and Preschoolers
Common Sense Parenting Learn-at-Home Video Kit
Angry Kids, Frustrated Parents
Dealing with Your Kids' 7 Biggest Troubles
Parents and Kids Talking About School Violence
Practical Tools for Foster Parents
Safe and Effective Secondary Schools
Teaching Social Skills to Youth
The Well-Managed Classroom
Unmasking Sexual Con Games
The Ongoing Journey
Journey of Faith
Journey of Hope
Journey of Love

For Adolescents
Boundaries: A Guide for Teens
A Good Friend
Who's in the Mirror?
What's Right for Me?

For a Boys Town Press catalog, call 1-800-282-6657.
www.girlsandboystown.org/btpress

Girls and Boys Town National Hotline
1-800-448-3000

**Parents can call the Girls and Boys Town
National Hotline with any problem at any time.**

PARENTING
To Build Character
In Your Teen

by
MICHAEL S. JOSEPHSON
VAL J. PETER
TOM DOWD

BOYS TOWN PRESS

BOYS TOWN, NEBRASKA

Parenting to Build Character in Your Teen

Published by the Boys Town Press
Father Flanagan's Boys' Home
Boys Town, NE 68010

Copyright © 2001 by Father Flanagan's Boys' Home

ISBN 1-889322-42-3

The Boys Town Press is the publishing division of Girls and Boys Town, the original Father Flanagan's Boys' Home.

Publisher's Cataloging-in-Publication
(Provided by Quality Books, Inc.)

Josephson, Michael S., 1942-

Parenting to build character in your teen / by Michael S. Josephson, Val J. Peter, and Tom Dowd. --1st ed.

p.cm.

Includes bibliographical references and index.

ISBN: 1-889322-42-3

1. Parent and teenager. 2. Teenagers--Conduct of life. 3. Moral education. 4. Character. 5. Parenting --Moral and ethical aspects. 6. Child rearing--Moral and ethical aspects. I. Peter, Val J. II. Dowd, Tom (Tom P.) III. Title.

HQ799.15.J67 2001   649'.125

QBI01-200258

10   9   8   7   6   5   4   3   2   1

Table of Contents

Introduction

Being a teenager is often stressful and confusing. But being the *parent* of a teenager sometimes seems impossible.

One minute, your son or daughter expects to be treated as an adult, but in the blink of an eye, is upset because you are expecting him or her to be too grown up.

Sometimes, teens don't know exactly who they are or who they want to be. When the caterpillar in Lewis Carroll's *Alice in Wonderland* asked Alice, "Who are you?" she gave the answer many teens might give. "I... I hardly know, sir, just at present. At least I knew who I was when I got up this morning, but I must have changed several times since then." Because of these seemingly endless changes, you probably find yourself feeling frustrated when you deal with your teenager.

Being the parent of a teenager can be like riding a roller-coaster. Some days, you're on top of the world because your kid took some initiative, was respectful or industrious, or otherwise made you proud. But other days, you feel like your teen has a long way to go toward becoming a full-fledged adult.

Always, you struggle to find a moment in your teen's hectic life of school activities, jobs, and friends just to spend time together. And you try not to fill those moments with "lectures" about cleaning his or her room or remembering to put gas in the car. And when you do want to talk about some of those BIG ISSUES like sex or drugs, you're not really sure how to start a conversation like that with your son or daughter.

> 'Character building begins in our infancy and continues until death.'
>
> – Eleanor Roosevelt

Believe it or not, your teenager is feeling confused too. It's just not easy being a teenager. While some big-picture trends for teenagers are more positive these days than in the past – student achievement levels have increased, teen pregnancy rates are down, and more kids are participating in community service work – the day-to-day issues about identity, friends, and the future still produce lots of uncertainty. And teenagers daily face enormous pressures to cheat in school, lie, use drugs and alcohol, and even engage in violence and other illegal or unhealthy activities.

The teenage years can be some of the most difficult you and your teen will experience. A teenager's job is to explore, experiment, and learn to express himself or herself and move into adulthood. That exploring, experimenting, and expressing may cause confusion and anxiety as everyone in the family learns new roles and responsibilities.

During this time, there's usually more conflict between you and your teen because both of you are dealing with new issues. Your teenager wants more independence and needs to "belong" with his or her crowd of friends. You have to start letting go of some of the control you have over your teen without letting go of the responsibilities of parenting. Both you and your teenager are dealing with the big issues like sex, drugs, driving, and curfews.

During these years, your teenager is developing new reasoning skills. Actually, the part of your teenager's brain that controls reasoning – the prefrontal cortex – is still developing and continues to develop until approximately age 20. That means your son or daughter's ability to use skills like self-control, judgment, emotional regulation, organization, and planning is not fully mature. Because of that, your teenager's decisions may not seem rational to you and may involve risks that you think are irresponsible and perhaps dangerous.

Some days, you may feel overwhelmed trying to adapt your parenting skills to the ever-changing world of your teenager. Maybe you're sick and tired of your teenager ignoring your advice, or worse yet, ridiculing it. Maybe you're tempted just to start counting the months until high school graduation or the day your son or daughter moves out. Maybe you've already experienced all those things.

You may be ready to give up. But you're not quite there yet. That's why you're reading this book. You want some fresh ideas to help guide your teenager in a world that is increasingly self-absorbed, cynical, and violent. In such a world, the teens who flourish are those with character and a solid set of values.

Both Girls and Boys Town and the CHARACTER COUNTS!™ Coalition work with kids and families every day to teach those lessons. With this book, they have joined forces to provide you with some powerful tools to help you instill good character and values in your teenager.

Our tools include Girls and Boys Town's Common Sense Parenting® program and CHARACTER COUNTS! Six Pillars of Character™ – trustworthiness, respect, responsibility, fairness, caring, and citizenship. This collaboration emphasizes a three-pronged approach to character building that focuses on the head, the heart, and habits. Let's talk a bit about what that means.

The Head

It has been said that character is essentially a matter of knowing the good, loving the good, and doing the good. So, building character in youngsters is a matter of teaching them to know the good (head), love the good (heart), and do the good (habits).

The "head" part refers to the intellectual aspects of being a good person. It focuses attention on things your teen ought to know and understand about the meaning and importance of good character and about trustworthiness, respect, responsibility, fairness, caring, and citizenship, the traits of good character.

In addition to learning how to identify and recognize conduct associated with good character, youth also should learn how to recognize the moral significance of their choices and to distinguish right from wrong by applying the ethical principles embodied in the Six Pillars of Character.

In addition, parents should help teens develop their reasoning skills by teaching them how to identify the people who are affected by their decisions, evaluate the possible consequences, and make sound moral judgments and decisions.

The Heart

The "heart" part of our strategy deals with the emotional and spiritual aspects of character. It involves ways of instilling in young people the durable and deep beliefs and values that help people lead a "good," meaningful life. Parents should help their teens develop a real appreciation for and love of the Six Pillars.

Focusing on the heart element of character development leads to the formation of a strong conscience that will guide young people throughout their lives, the kind of moral roots that let these soon-to-be adults look at themselves unflinchingly in the mirror every morning.

Habits

Concentrating on "habits" involves conduct and a parent's responsibility to reinforce good behavior and attitudes so strongly that they become automatic and instinctive. Just as children learn to say "Please" and "Thank you" when their parents expect and demand this conduct, they can learn other forms of ethical conduct and make them a permanent part of their lives.

Throughout this book, we'll talk a lot about teaching. As parents, we are our kids' first teachers. Even during the teenage years, when we think our ability to influence our kids has dwindled, they still look to us and learn from us. The lessons they learn may be good and moral or not. It's up to us.

With this book, we hope to help you become a better teacher, to identify teaching opportunities when they occur naturally, and through that teaching, to give your teenagers the skills they need.

This book is for parents who have built a solid relationship with their kids but want some new, practical ways to communicate, teach, and reinforce the essential character Pillars. Most importantly, it's for parents who want some help in identifying and setting character development goals for their kids, and then learning how to reach those goals.

Some parents might question whether using our teaching to instill positive character traits will interfere with their family's basic beliefs, including beliefs about religion. There's no need to worry. Girls and Boys Town and CHARACTER COUNTS! are devoted to making kids' lives better, not changing anyone's basic belief structure or supporting any one religious belief system over another. We believe our teaching can dovetail nicely with any religious faith. Or you may simply use the tools we've developed along with your family's own core beliefs.

We believe that the power of a loving parent is one of the most potent forces on earth. Sometimes, the stress of a long, frustrating day may make you forget what your teen has accomplished because of you. No, you're not ready to give up. We believe you can do even more to help your teenager become a good person. We believe the best is yet to come.

CHAPTER 1

An Overview

*Romance fails us and so do friendships, but the
relationship of parent and teen remains indelible and
indestructible, the strongest relationship on earth.*

– THEODORE REIK

*The pressures of being a parent are equal to any
pressure on earth. To be a conscious parent, and
really look to that little being's mental and physical
health, is a responsibility which most of us, including
me, avoid most of the time because it's too hard.
To put it loosely, the reason why kids are crazy is
because nobody can face the responsibility of
bringing them up.*

– JOHN LENNON

With this book, two of America's leading child-oriented organizations join forces to create a toolbox of skills specifically designed for parents of teenagers.

Girls and Boys Town and the CHARACTER COUNTS! Coalition have different organizational missions, but at the heart of both organizations is the commitment to make the world a better place for kids. We think you'll find that the parenting tools forged from our partnership give you practical help with the teenagers in your life.

The Girls and Boys Town Story

For more than a decade, Girls and Boys Town's Common Sense Parenting program has been helping mothers and fathers around the country and the world find success at the most important job in the world – being a good parent.

Using our experience from 80-plus years of caring for young people at the Village of Boys Town near Omaha and, in the last two decades, at 18 sites around the country, we have developed a research-based, outcome-oriented system that helps parents build closer relationships with their children and reduce problems by teaching youngsters appropriate ways to behave.

In the decade since Common Sense Parenting classes began, we have provided training for thousands of parents, as well as representatives of children's service agencies, counseling centers, churches, and schools. In addition, we've sold more than 100,000 copies of the book, *Common Sense Parenting*.

Common Sense Parenting is based on the belief that people can become better parents by developing solid relationships with their children, teaching instead of punishing, and using other practical skills that bring about positive results. COMMON SENSE PARENTING techniques combined with CHARACTER COUNTS! values provide you with a toolbox of strategies that help you teach your teenagers not only the social skills they need to find success in the world, but also the beliefs and values that will help them to be good people.

Girls and Boys Town's founder Father Edward Flanagan believed that teaching kids those values and beliefs provided them with the moral compass they needed to navigate in a complicated and confusing world. Father Flanagan also believed that good people can make the world a better place, and he stressed that lesson for kids from the first day he opened his home for boys in 1917.

"If we want to live in a good world, then we must help make it that kind of world by our acts and prayers," Father Flanagan said. "If we want good will to reign, then we must see first that we are people of good will." (You can learn more about Girls and Boys Town on the Internet at **www.girlsandboystown.org**.)

The CHARACTER COUNTS! Story

The CHARACTER COUNTS! Coalition is a project of the nonprofit Joseph & Edna Josephson Institute of Ethics, established in 1993.

The CHARACTER COUNTS! Coalition is a diverse partnership of nearly 500 organizations involved in the education, training, and care of youth and society. Comprised of many school districts, municipalities, service organizations, and business groups, this alliance works to improve the character of America's young people by promoting consensus ethical values called the "Six Pillars of Character."

The Six Pillars – trustworthiness, respect, responsibility, fairness, caring, and citizenship – form the basis of a growing number of age-appropriate curricular and awareness materials. The Pillars are described in more detail on the next page.

Training is designed for teachers, school administrators, youth group leaders, social agency organizers, and community leaders. The training focus is directed toward designing character-building activities that can be integrated into existing curricula, extracurricular activities, and sports programs. This approach allows educators to respond effectively to challenges and questions from students, parents, and colleagues. Instruction in the Six Pillars of Character provides a powerful means of overcoming unwelcome trends prevalent in today's society.

Schools, service organizations, and youth programs that have received CHARACTER COUNTS! training have experienced tremendous results, including decreases in disciplinary referrals, classroom disruptions, and fighting. Increased attentiveness and improvements in classroom participation and tolerance also have been reported. (You can learn more about CHARACTER COUNTS! on the Internet at **www.charactercounts.org**.)

The Six Pillars of Character

At the heart of the CHARACTER COUNTS! Program are its Six Pillars of Character, which provide the framework for values education. The Pillars are defined here.

Trustworthiness: Be honest. Don't deceive, cheat, or steal. Be reliable – do what you say you'll do. Have the courage to do the right thing. Build a good reputation. Be loyal – stand by your family, friends, and country.

Respect: Treat others with respect; follow the Golden Rule. Be tolerant of differences. Use good manners, not bad language. Be considerate of the feelings of others. Don't threaten, hit, or hurt anyone. Deal peacefully with anger, insults, and disagreements.

Responsibility: Do what you are supposed to do. Persevere; keep on trying! Always do your best. Use self-control. Be self-disciplined. Think before you act – consider the consequences. Be accountable for your choices.

Fairness: Play by the rules. Take turns and share. Be open-minded; listen to others. Don't take advantage of others. Don't blame others carelessly.

Caring: Be kind. Be compassionate and show you care. Express gratitude. Forgive others. Help people in need.

Citizenship: Do your share to make your school and community better. Cooperate. Stay informed; vote. Be a good neighbor. Obey laws and rules. Respect authority. Protect the environment.

Parenting and Character

No relationship carries more moral responsibility than the parent-teen relationship. One of the chief responsibilities of parents to both their children and to society is to instill positive values, teach responsibility, and promote good character. Another is to look out for the well-being of those children, be attentive to what they are saying and doing, and try to understand what they are feeling and needing.

The idea that parents have a moral duty to develop the character of their children has deep roots. The Bible (Proverbs 22:6) instructs parents to "Train up a child in the way he should go, and when he is old he shall not depart from it."

Poet Kahlil Gibran says that parents are the "bows" from which "children, as living arrows, are sent forth."

Parents should make a conscious choice about the values they want to instill in their children and look for opportunities to emphasize and model behaviors that they think are worthy of admiration.

But parents are not responsible for everything their children do. Many people of great character have emerged from morally impoverished childhoods, and some people who have committed horrendous acts against humanity have come out of theoretically model homes.

While we can't guarantee that our kids will become everything we want them to be, if we try to teach them positive values and habits, they are more likely to adopt those values and habits in their adult lives and contribute to the greater good. In that sense, says sociologist Amitai Etzioni, parents have a moral responsibility to the community:

"Making a child is a moral act. Obviously, it obligates the parents to the child. But it also obligates the parents to the community. We must all live with the consequences of children who are not brought up properly.... Juvenile delinquents do more than break their parents' hearts, and drug abusers do more than give their parents grief. They mug the elderly, hold up stores and gas stations, and prey on innocent children returning from school. They grow up to be problems, draining society's resources and patience. In contrast, well-brought-up children are more than a joy to their families; they are (oddly, it is necessary to reiterate this) a foundation of proud and successful communities."

The Nature of Character

When we talk about teaching character lessons to our kids, we're really talking about teaching the three essential qualities associated with good character:

First, people of character have **good principles**. They believe in honor, integrity, duty, compassion, justice, and other ethical values. Those principles are summarized in the Six Pillars of Character.

Second, people of character possess a **strong conscience**. Conscience is an internal moral compass that helps us know right from wrong, and a virtuous inner voice that constantly reminds us of our moral obligations, urging us to live up to them. A strong conscience will not be denied. It enforces its moral judgments by rewarding good behavior with good feelings of pride and self-esteem. It also imposes penalties for bad behavior in the form of shame and guilt.

Third, people of character have **moral courage,** the willpower to listen to that inner voice and do the right thing, even when it's costly, risky, or unpleasant. Good character, then, is also moral or ethical strength.

We also need to teach our teenagers that character is not predetermined or inborn. It is built day by day in the values we live and the choices we make. Each one of us builds our own character, and we make conscious choices to make our characters stronger or weaker.

Each day we can decide to change our attitudes, re-evaluate and re-rank our values, and exercise a higher level of self-control to change our behavior. Character is the cause of our actions, but it is also the result of our actions.

Aristotle said, "We are what we repeatedly do." The power to control our actions is the power to control our character, and the power to control our character is the power to control our lives.

In this book, we'll take an in-depth look at each of the Six Pillars of Character and show how you can use proven tools from Girls and Boys Town to help your teenagers become adults of character.

CHAPTER 2

The TEAM Approach to Parenting

Tackling something as complex and important as character-building requires a game plan: a practical, realistic strategy to help parents use all the ideas, techniques, and advice suggested in this book. CHARACTER COUNTS! uses the acronym TEAM to help parents achieve their goals by zeroing in on four distinct methods of character development. TEAM stands for:

Teach

Enforce

Advocate

Model

This chapter will provide an explanation of each element of the TEAM concept, along with the Girls and Boys Town Common Sense Parenting tools that you can use to help your kids develop the character traits that will make them adults of principle. We'll use the TEAM con-

17

cept throughout the book as a guideline for your discussions with your teenagers.

Teach

The first step in the TEAM approach is to teach your teenagers what it means to have good character, that character truly does count, and that their success and happiness in life will depend on whom they are inside, not on what they have or how they look.

Does that seem like a huge undertaking? Where do you begin to teach big issues like character and morals? You can start by using six basic rules of living (the Six Pillars of Character): trustworthiness, respect, responsibility, fairness, caring, and good citizenship.

As early as possible, teach your kids what these words mean. Help your kids understand that people of character know the difference between right and wrong because they know what these six basic words mean. Use examples from your own life, history, and the news.

> 'Character isn't inherited. One builds it daily by the way one thinks and acts, thought by thought, action by action.'
>
> – HELEN GAHAGAN DOUGLAS

We believe that parents are their children's first teachers and that parents should continue that teaching as children grow into teenagers. In this book, we'll discuss some of the teaching methods parents learn in Girls and Boys Town Common Sense Parenting classes. A brief outline of those methods is presented here; in later chapters, we'll talk in more detail about how you can use these tools to teach your teenager many lessons, including the Six Pillars of Character.

Effective Praise combines praise, reasons, and positive consequences to reinforce a specific behavior. You can use *Effective Praise* any time you notice your teenager doing something good, such as helping clear the dinner table without being asked or reaching out to a classmate in friendship.

Preventive Teaching is a way to prevent problems by teaching teens what to do and having them practice before they encounter a specific situation. *Preventive Teaching* works best when a youngster is learning something new or when he or she has had difficulty in the past. For example, you might use *Preventive Teaching* to talk to your teenager about how to say "No" if he or she is being pressured by peers to drink.

Corrective Teaching helps you identify your teenager's inappropriate behaviors and guide him or her to more appropriate ways of behaving. You can use a form of *Corrective Teaching* called *Guided Self-Correction* when your teenager has made a bad choice and needs to fix a problem he or she has created.

Teaching Self-Control helps you and your teenager remain in control of emotions in situations where someone is angry or upset.

Enforce

Enforcing character means regularly finding opportunities to talk to your teenager about character – the moral obligations they face and the moral significance of the choices they make.

Enforcing character also means reinforcing your teenagers for the character choices they make – offering praise for good choices and imposing consequences for choices not rooted in principle.

Finally, enforcing character involves showing your kids what it means to stick to their values when it is difficult or costly for them to do so. Remember: Actions speak louder than words.

Advocate

Being an advocate for character means continuously encouraging teens to live up to the Six Pillars of Character in all their thoughts and actions.

Advocating character means being relentlessly gung-ho about the power of character to shape lives for the better. It means talking to your kids about the reasons why they should embrace qualities embodied in the Six Pillars of Character, even in the most mundane situation. For example, wiping your feet before you come into the house shows that you care about your home and other members of the family.

Advocating character means never being neutral about the importance of character or casual about improper conduct. It means being clear and uncompromising in your expectation that your children be trustworthy, respectful, responsible, fair, caring, and good citizens.

Model

"He's a chip off the old block."

"The apple never falls too far from the tree."

"Like father, like son" or *"Like mother, like daughter."*

All of these sayings have one thing in common: They refer to the phenomenon of children learning and imitating the behaviors and personality characteristics of their parents.

Your children started watching and listening to you when they were very young, and the watching and listening continues well into the teen years. Many parents think their teenagers no longer hear what they say, but interviews and surveys of teens consistently show that they still look to their parents for guidance.

Be careful and self-conscious about setting a good example in everything you say and do. Hold yourself to the highest standards of character by honoring the Six Pillars of Character at all times.

You may be a good model now, but remember, you don't have to be sick to get better. Everything you do, and don't do, sends a message to your teenagers about your values. Be sure your messages reinforce your lessons about doing the right thing, even when it is hard to do. When you slip (and all of us do), act the way you want your children to behave when they act improperly – be accountable, apologize sincerely, and work to do better.

Modeling is not something most parents consciously do. In fact, as a parent, you are modeling behavior for your teen all the time. That's why it's so important that your behaviors are consistent with the behavior you expect from your teen. For example, let's say you're driving your teen to school when another driver cuts you off in traffic. You curse and swear, then shake your fist at the offender when you catch up to him at the next traffic light. If the next time you're riding with your teen, you see him or her use the same aggressive behaviors toward other drivers, it's going to be very difficult to explain why it's wrong and inappropriate.

The same goes for modeling positive behaviors. For example, returning the extra change the store cashier gave you by mistake when you and your teen were shopping models honesty. If you witness your teen respond in the same way in a similar situation, you'll know that he or she has learned a valuable lesson from your actions.

TEAM and Character

Think about the teaching, enforcing, advocating, and modeling you can do with your teenager as you begin to work with the concepts of character and values. In the next four chapters, we'll introduce the skills of the Girls and Boys Town's Common Sense Parenting program. In later chapters, we'll discuss each of the Six Pillars of Character, and we'll show you how to use Common Sense Parenting skills to teach your teenager those Pillars.

CHAPTER 3

Encouraging Character with Praise

Showing your kids you care about them is an important part of being a parent. But it can be difficult with busy teenagers who spend more time with friends than with you.

Praise – focusing on the things your kids do well, or the efforts they make to improve – is a great way to show your kids that you care about them and provides vital emotional nourishment during the turbulent teen years.

As important as praise is, we don't give our kids nearly enough of it. That's because, as parents, we often focus on the mistakes our kids make. Mistakes tend to capture our attention in a negative way because they require us to take some action, like visiting the vice-principal when our children misbehave at school.

It takes some effort to start focusing on the good things your kids do, but you'll find that praise truly works wonders. If you consistently praise your teenagers, as well as offer nurturing and reinforcing words, actions like pats on the back, or high-fives, and whatever positive feedback feels right and is motivating to your teenager, you will notice dramatic improvements over time. When you zero in on as many positive things about your kids as you can, your kids will feel better about themselves, and they'll also feel cared for and loved.

> 'We increase whatever we praise. The whole creation responds to praise and is glad.'
>
> – Charles Fillmore

You can use praise and nurturing behaviors with your teenagers in these three basic situations: for things your kids already do well, for improvements in behavior, and for positive attempts they make at learning new skills.

The easiest way to praise someone is to say things like, *"Fantastic,"* or *"Keep up the good work."* This is called general praise. It's a quick and easy way to focus on the positive things your kids do. These words show your affection and approval and really encourage your kids to do well. In addition, praise just makes kids feel good.

Effective Praise

But you can make general praise even better by using what Girls and Boys Town calls *Effective Praise.*

Effective Praise is a more specific kind of praise than general praise. In *Effective Praise,* you combine praise with a specific description of the good behavior you see your teenager doing.

24

Here are some examples of how *Effective Praise* might sound to reinforce some Pillars of Character:

"Way to go, Rashawn! You made your curfew! You showed me that I can trust you to keep your word! "

"Eric, I noticed that you held the door open for that lady at the mall. That was a caring thing to do!"

Effective Praise has three steps. They are:

1. Show your approval.

2. Describe the positive behavior.

3. Give a reason.

Let's take a quick look at what each step means.

1. Show your approval.

There are lots of ways to tell your teenager that you approve of something he or she did. *"Awesome!" "That's right!" "I'm impressed!" "Way to go!"* are just a few. You'll think of others. Remember to be enthusiastic (and mean it!) when you show approval, and try to vary the words you use. Too often parents say things like, *"Good job!"* every time they praise their kids, and that phrase quickly loses its impact.

Another way to show your approval is with actions like "high-fives," a "thumbs up" gesture, or a wink and a smile. Hugs and kisses work, too, but some teenagers find such demonstrations of affection embarrassing. Use whatever gestures you know will be meaningful and acceptable to your teenager.

25

Showing your approval lets kids know that you're excited about what they're doing well. In turn, they will be more satisfied with themselves.

2. Describe the positive behavior.

After you show your kids approval, describe the specific behaviors you liked. Make sure your kids understand what they did well so they'll be able to repeat the behavior in the future. Praise what you just saw or heard your teenager do well. For example, say, *"Joe, thanks for filling up the car with gas."*

3. Give a reason.

Teenagers benefit from knowing why a behavior is helpful to them or others. It helps them understand the relationship between their behavior and what happens to them.

For example, if your teenager volunteers to clean up the family room before guests arrive (and then does it), explain why that behavior is helpful. For example, say, *"Cleaning up the family room really saved us a lot of time. Now we have time to get everything finished before the dinner party."*

Or you could say, *"Since you helped out, I'll have time to take you over to Jenna's house before the party. I don't know if I would have had time if you hadn't helped."*

When you give a reason, you also can mention a Pillar if it's applicable to the situation. For example, *"I'm impressed, Marina! You showed a lot of responsibility by getting your college application mailed a week early!"*

Giving your teenager a reason links his or her behavior to the consequences or outcomes of that behavior. Reasons are particularly valuable when they can demonstrate the benefits your teen may receive, either immediately or in the future.

> **'I praise loudly, I blame softly.'**
>
> – CATHERINE THE GREAT

Make sure the reasons you use are brief, believable, age-appropriate, and teen-related (important in your teen's world).

Here are some descriptions of teen behaviors and corresponding teen-related reasons that some parents have given:

- *"It's important to accept criticism from your teacher so that he knows that you're taking responsibility for the mistakes on your homework. When you do that, he'll be more likely to help you with the problems in the future."*

- *"When you tell me the truth about where you're going, I will trust you more and probably will let you go out more often."*

- *"When you show me you can respect the house rules, I'll be more likely to let you do more things with your friends."*

Helpful Hints

Effective Praise works because it lets kids know exactly what they're doing right. Because of that, they're more likely to repeat those behaviors. Below are some tips for using *Effective Praise:*

Praise small accomplishments as well as large ones.

Don't reserve your praise for your teenager's major life accomplishments like winning the state football championship or getting the lead in the school play. Kids do great things every day. If you notice your son putting his dirty lunch dishes in the dishwasher instead of leaving them on the counter, praise that. If your daughter (who usually runs late) is ready to leave for school five minutes early, let her know you noticed her effort.

Be sure to tie praise to specific behavior.

Some parents tell us that their praise doesn't seem to mean much to their kids. That's probably because they're praising kids for everything. If you use praise selectively, it will mean more to kids.

Give rewards occasionally.

You might want to reward your teenager for something he or she did especially well. The reward might be something tangible, like a gift, or a privilege, such as extending a curfew. The reward also can be as simple as a hearty pat on the back or an enthusiastic high-five.

Parents who've consistently used *Effective Praise* tell us that using praise and nurturing their children have had a lasting impact on their families. Parents find themselves being more positive about their kids, and kids, in turn, are more positive about their parents. With *Effective Praise,* everyone wins.

CHAPTER 4

Preventing Problems Before They Occur

Sometimes, we forget that our teenagers still have some learning to do. They may seem so grown up, yet not have a clue about some basic life skills.

That's where the Girls and Boys Town teaching method called *Preventive Teaching* comes in. *Preventive Teaching* is teaching your teenager what he or she will need to know for a future situation and practicing it in advance.

Preventive Teaching gives you a systematic approach to doing this teaching with your kids. The steps of *Preventive Teaching* are:

1. **Describe what the youth needs to know.**

2. **Give a reason.**

3. **Practice.**

We'll discuss these steps in detail later in this chapter.

When to Use Preventive Teaching

There are two types of situations where you can use *Preventive Teaching:*

- When your teenager is learning something new.
- When your teenager has had difficulty in a past situation.

New situations for teenagers may include filling out a job application, asking an employer for a raise, asking someone for a date, registering to vote, etc.

Situations from the past that have proved difficult may include using good sportsmanship at an athletic event, telling the truth, giving a speech, etc.

In each case, remember to use *Preventive Teaching* **before the situation** so you maximize your teenager's chances for success. *Preventive Teaching* is a simple concept, but parents usually don't use it as often or in as many situations as they could. Keep in mind that it's easier (and less frustrating) to teach your teenager something a few times before there is a problem than to repeatedly correct him or her for doing something wrong.

Steps of Preventive Teaching

Let's look at the steps of *Preventive Teaching.* Then we'll discuss some scenarios that describe how you can use *Preventive Teaching* to teach some of the Pillars of Character.

Here's a look at how the steps work:

1. Describe what the youth needs to know.

Before your teenagers know what to do, they must first know what is expected of them in certain situations. Talk to them about those expectations. Be specific and make sure your teenagers understand what they're supposed to do.

With most of the teaching you do, it's important to guide teens to finding answers on their own, but in some situations, it's equally important for you to give them specific information that they may not have. This is especially true when they face a new situation.

They may not know, for example, what information to bring with them to complete a job application. Or they may not know how to approach their boss to resolve a conflict at work involving a co-worker. Find out how much your teenager knows about an upcoming situation and determine if he or she has a good idea how to handle it. Then you can provide the right amount of assistance without lecturing.

2. Give a reason.

Teenagers, like adults, benefit from knowing why they should act a certain way. When you give your teenager reasons why they should do something or behave in a certain way, they are better able to understand how their actions affect not only what happens to them, but also what happens to other people.

If teenagers know they are learning something that will benefit them, they will be much more open to the teaching and remember more of it.

Try to make the reason you give meaningful to your teenager and relevant to his or her life. For example, telling your son that he'll be able to focus more on his game if he's not angry at the referee may be more motivating than telling him that society frowns on people who get angry.

Keep in mind that your teenagers may not always agree with your reason, but they will at least know why you think something is important.

3. Practice.

Knowing what to do and knowing how to do it are two different things. Any new skill needs to be practiced. You can tell your daughter how to safely drive a car, but she'll be a lot better driver if she's practiced in a driver education class.

Getting teenagers to practice something can be challenging. They may feel embarrassed by practicing or think it's a waste of time. But you can make the practice more effective with teenagers by setting it up with words like, *"Show me how you would handle..."* or *"Okay, in the same type of situation, what would you say to..."* This gives teenagers an opportunity to demonstrate their abilities without feeling like you are talking down to them.

After finishing the practice, praise areas that your teenager did well in and offer encouragement in areas that need improvement. Don't expect perfection the first time your teen practices. He or she can practice again if necessary.

If you are helping your teen practice a complex skill or a difficult situation, such as how to say "No" to peer pressure or using drugs, never promise that the actual situation will work out perfectly. Emphasize to your son or daughter that he or she is practicing *possible ways* to handle the situation and the outcome won't always be the same as the one you practice. You cannot ensure your teenager's success in every situation; you can only improve the odds.

> 'It is easier to prevent bad habits than to break them.'
>
> – BENJAMIN FRANKLIN

Also remember that the more types of situations you can practice with your teenagers, the more likely they are to succeed in the actual situations. You will be helping them learn more and more ways to solve problems.

Responsibility: Being a Good Sport

Situation: Your son is on the varsity basketball team. He is short-tempered and tends to argue with referees. A big game is coming up and you want to help your son keep his temper under control so he won't yell at a referee and risk getting thrown out of the game, which happened earlier in the season.

Describe what he needs to know: Tell him that you know the upcoming game is an important one. Ask him what ideas he has about ways to keep his temper under control. If he hasn't thought of any, help him think of some.

Give a reason: Explain that he owes it to his teammates to keep his temper under control. He also owes it to himself so he can play his best and not let anger short-circuit his focus.

Practice: Have your son practice his self-control methods. You can play the part of the referee making a call your son doesn't like. Your son then can do whatever works best for him, such as walking away from the referee, counting to ten, telling himself to calm down, etc.

Citizenship: Voting for the First Time

Situation: Your daughter has just become eligible to vote.

Describe what she needs to know: Talk to your teenager about how to register to vote. Have her call the county election commissioner's office to find out how the registration process works. Make sure you start this process well in advance of any upcoming election. Also, make sure your daughter knows where she is supposed to go to vote.

Talk to your daughter about political parties and how they work, what resources she can use to stay informed about ballot issues, and the importance of critical listening when it comes to candidate speeches.

Give a reason: Emphasize the importance of voting, being informed, and making thoughtful decisions about candidates and issues.

Practice: Some newspapers run sample ballots before an election. Have your daughter review them and fill them out before she goes to the polling place for the first time.

Preventive Prompts

After using *Preventive Teaching* several times to teach a skill, you may only need to provide a reminder – a preventive prompt – when your teen needs to use that skill. For example, let's say that you have helped your son practice how to keep his temper under control with referees. Before he leaves for the basketball game, you could say, *"Remember to walk away if you find yourself getting mad."* The purpose of a preventive prompt is to get your teenager focused on what you have practiced.

Summary

Preventive Teaching is a valuable tool for both parents and teenagers. You can promote gradual behavior changes in areas where your teenagers may be having problems and help them prepare for unfamiliar situations. *Preventive Teaching* can increase teenagers' self-confidence by showing them that they can learn how to change behaviors and be successful. And, perhaps most importantly, *Preventive Teaching* allows you and your teen to work toward goals together. Taking the time to be with your teen and showing him or her that you care helps improve relationships, and that benefits the whole family.

CHAPTER 5

Helping Teens Correct Their Own Behavior

One way to reinforce the Pillars of Character is to correct your teenagers when they behave inappropriately or make poor choices. When you hear the word "correct," you may think about a good old-fashioned lecture or traditional scolding. These may be successful in some situations, but a better way to help teenagers correct their behaviors is a Girls and Boys Town teaching method called *Guided Self-Correction.*

Asking Questions

Guided Self-Correction encourages teenagers to be more active participants in correcting a situation. In *Guided Self-Correction,* you ask a series of questions to get your teenager to think about a situation and determine why a behavior or decision was inappropriate.

By answering those questions, teens can demonstrate that they know what they did wrong and can use problem-solving skills to correct the situation. This is an excellent way for them to begin honing their reasoning skills, the "head" part of the head-heart-habits triad we described earlier.

Here's how *Guided Self-Correction* might sound:

"Matt, your boss called here looking for you this afternoon. I told him you were at basketball camp and I said that I thought you'd asked for the afternoon off. He sounded kind of mad. What happened?"

"I asked him two weeks ago and he said, 'Okay.' I guess he forgot I wasn't going to be around."

"Why do you think he got mad?"

"Well it must have been busy, and then I didn't show up."

"What could you have done to be more responsible so he wouldn't have spent time looking for you?"

"I guess I should have reminded him, but I didn't think about that. I'll call him and apologize."

"Good thinking. That will show him that you can take responsibility."

Guided Self-Correction works well with teenagers because it challenges them to be accountable and to solve problems for themselves. It works well for parents because it provides them a way to teach and correct without preaching or nagging.

How to Ask Questions

To help your teenager use *Guided Self-Correction*, ask general questions first to establish what the problem is. Then, ask more specific questions to determine whether your teenager is using faulty thinking (poor logic: *"I wasn't going that fast! It was only ten miles over the speed limit!"*) or distorted thinking (a pattern of thinking that processes information with a bias: *"I got a speeding ticket because that cop was out to get me 'cause I'm a teenager!"*).

As you begin this process of asking questions, remember: Don't offer answers to the questions. That's what your teenager is supposed to do. Also, ask the questions in a nonthreatening manner, and give your teen time to think about answers.

For example, your first question might be a simple *"What happened?"* With that question, you ask teenagers to describe the situation in which they find themselves. Essentially, you are asking them to take the first step toward recognizing that they did something wrong, but your tone is not accusatory. You simply ask them to describe the situation in an effort to get them to see their role in it.

After some general questions, you can get more specific, honing in on the nuts and bolts of the situation to determine your teen's thinking. Ask questions like these:

- *"Why do you think he got mad?"*
- *"What would you have done if you were in his position?"*
- *"What can you do now that might make things better?"*

- *"What would be a positive solution to this problem?"*

Working Toward a Solution

With these questions, you guide your teenager toward a solution to the problem and an understanding of his or her part in the situation, as well as an opportunity to "walk in someone else's shoes." Your teenager's answers to these questions also will give you an idea whether his or her reasoning is sound or distorted.

For example, in the earlier example, the parent asked her teenager why he thinks the boss got mad when he didn't show up for work. The youth answered that the place where he worked must have been busy and needed him to help out. That's sound reasoning.

> 'All men make mistakes, but only wise men learn from their mistakes.'
>
> – SIR WINSTON CHURCHILL

But if the teenager had answered that the boss always picks on him and must be out to get him, the parent would know that the teenager was using distorted thinking. The parent then could test her son's reasoning processes by asking her son why he felt that way and what evidence he had to back up his reasoning.

The parent could determine if her son had valid reasons for thinking the boss had a vendetta against him. If there didn't appear to be valid reasons, she could use questions to teach her son that he wasn't using sound reasoning and that he wasn't making a true connection

between what happened and how his employer respond-
ed. Those questions might include:

- *"You said your boss picks on you. What do you mean by that?"*
- *"What are you usually doing before he begins to pick on you?"*
- *"What does he say to you?"*
- *"What do you say to him?"*
- *"Does he pick on other people who work there?"*
- *"What are they usually doing before he begins to pick on them?"*
- *"Why do you think he is picking on you?"*
- *"If you could trade places with your boss, what would you say about the work you are doing there?"*
- *"Are there things you could do differently at work that might make him stop picking on you?"*

When you help teenagers see the connections between their behaviors and the situations they find themselves in, they begin to realize that they have the power to solve problems and will want to apply their ideas to other prob-lem-solving situations. Teens become self-directed and accountable for their behaviors.

Using *Guided Self-Correction* also helps you avoid lecturing to your kids, which we all know is not a suc-cessful way to teach teenagers.

In addition, *Guided Self-Correction* is an exception-ally good tool for teaching the Six Pillars of Character because you can use the Pillars in your questioning process to help your teen identify the problem in a broad-er way. In the earlier example, for instance, the parent used "responsibility" in reference to the son's failure to remind his boss that he was taking time off from work.

Keep in mind that using *Guided Self-Correction* is a gradual process, and that you may have to prompt your teenager using open-ended questions to make him aware of the reasoning process he's using and how his behavior can result in certain consequences.

Helpful Hints

Here are some tips for using *Guided Self-Correction:*

Ask questions.

Begin your Guided Self-Correction teaching by ask-ing general, non-threatening questions such as *"What happened?"* or *"Let's talk about what's going on here."*

Have your teen describe the behavior.

The questions you ask should prompt your teenager to describe his or her behavior or the situation he or she is in. This is the first step toward correcting the problem.

Help your teen see whether his or her reasoning is sound.

If your teenager's answers to your questions don't indicate to you that he or she is using sound reasoning, take time to talk about his or her reasoning process and how the reasons connect to the situation.

Vary your questions.

After your teen has described the situation, ask more specific questions to focus in on the problem.

Encourage your teen to take ownership of the problem.

As the discussion continues, ask questions about what action your teenager can take to solve the problem. That's a good foundation for him or her to take ownership of the problem as well as its solution.

Help your teenager connect behaviors and outcomes.

As your teenager takes ownership of the problem, he or she should begin to see connections between what he or she did and what happened in the situation.

Help your teenager apply ideas to other settings.

As teenagers learn to make connections and to take ownership of problems, they should be able to adapt their problem-solving skills to other situations.

Talk it out.

Remember that your role in *Guided Self-Correction* is to talk out the problem with your teenager, not solve the problem.

Use empathy and encouragement.

Using empathy and encouragement shows your teen that you care about him or her and that you have faith in your teen's ability to change inappropriate behaviors and make good decisions.

CHAPTER 6

Teaching Self-Control to Teens

When you're the parent of a young child, you take charge of a situation where your child loses self-control. For example, if your 2-year-old daughter has a tantrum in the grocery store, you get her calmed down and teach her that throwing a tantrum is not appropriate behavior.

But when your teenager loses self-control, society expects that teenager to be able to calm himself or herself down. If that doesn't happen, the stakes can be pretty high. Your teenager may harm someone if his or her bad temper turns physical, or he or she may jeopardize a friendship with a torrent of angry words.

A Survival Skill

Self-control is one of the most important lessons you will teach your son or daughter. It is nothing less than a survival skill, because the inability to control emotions – the "heart" part of our head-heart-habits formula – can mean struggling with every aspect of living in society,

47

including having successful relationships with others and holding down a job. And mastering self-control is an essential ingredient to a teen making the Six Pillars of Character part of his or her everyday life.

Teaching a teenager to control his or her emotions can be a trying experience, but it is a necessary part of parenting and helping your child grow up. Your son or daughter relies on you to teach those lessons, which often grow out of a conflict between you and your kids. Kids must learn that negative, aggressive, and dishonest behavior is not acceptable. It is irresponsible and it is harmful to them and others. The sooner kids learn to control their actions, the more they will benefit.

> 'If you are patient in one moment of anger, you will escape a hundred days of sorrow.'
>
> – CHINESE PROVERB

Girls and Boys Town has developed a method called *Teaching Self-Control* that can help parents teach their kids a better way to respond when they get upset.

When to Use Teaching Self-Control

When a parent and a teenager have a conflict, a great deal of talking by the parent does little to improve the situation. Often, the more the parent talks, the more the teen talks back or yells. The more the teen yells, the louder the parent talks, until the parent is yelling too. This unpleasant exchange continues to intensify until someone decides that the argument is too painful and drops out. It can be the parent, who walks out of the room in disgust and anger. Or it can be the teenager, who stomps off to the bedroom and slams the door shut or runs out of the house. In either case, the problem has gotten worse, not better. If you've had to deal with a situation like this, you know how angry and helpless you can feel at these emotionally intense times.

Teaching Self-Control gives parents a way to stop the yelling or arguing before it gets harmful, before problems get worse. *Teaching Self-Control* gives parents a method for helping their kids identify how they're feeling and helping them learn how to deal with these behaviors in ways that are helpful, not harmful.

You can use *Teaching Self-Control* in two types of situations:

1. When your teenager does something wrong and will not respond to your efforts to correct him or her; instead the misbehavior continues or gets worse.

2. When your teenager "blows up" – a sudden and intense emotional outburst – and refuses to do anything that you ask.

Steps of Teaching Self-Control

The first part of *Teaching Self-Control – Calming Down –* is geared toward decreasing the intensity of your interaction so that both you and your teen can work together to resolve the disagreement.

The second part of *Teaching Self-Control* is *Follow-Up Teaching*. It gives you an opportunity to teach your teen some acceptable ways of behaving – some options – when he or she is upset. Like the other Girls and Boys Town skills, *Teaching Self-Control* emphasizes giving clear descriptions of your teen's behaviors, using consequences, and teaching your teen the correct behavior.

Part One: Calming Down

1. **Describe the problem behavior.**

2. **Give clear instructions.**

3. **Allow time to calm down.**

Part Two: Follow-Up Teaching

1. **Describe what your teen could do differently next time.**

2. **Have your teen practice what he or she can do next time.**

3. **Give a consequence.**

Teaching Self-Control gives both you and your kids a chance to calm down after tempers have flared. Allowing time to calm down before continuing your teaching increases the likelihood that your kids will have learned to share their feelings in constructive ways. Let's take a look at the steps of *Teaching Self-Control* and an explanation of each.

Part One: Calming Down

1. Describe the problem behavior.

Briefly tell your teenager what he or she is doing wrong. We emphasize "briefly" here. Your son or daughter is not always interested in listening to what you have to say at this time, so saying a lot won't help. Be clear and specific in what you say. Use a calm, level voice tone. Don't speak too rapidly or try to say too much. For example, *"Marcus, you're yelling at me and pacing around the room,"* gives the youth a clear message about what he is doing.

Parents often say judgmental things when they dislike their teen's behavior. They might say, for example, *"Quit acting like a baby,"* or *"You have a lousy attitude."* But these vague or judgmental statements don't help your teenager understand what's wrong; they only fuel the emotional fire in him or her. We suggest that you simply describe what your teen is doing wrong without becoming angry, sarcastic, or accusatory.

It also helps to use empathy, to show your son or daughter that you understand how he or she is feeling. For instance, you might say, *"I know you are upset right now. And, I know you're unhappy with what happened."* This adds a positive tone to your teaching, and shows your teen that you really do care about his or her feelings. Plus, using empathy often helps you focus on your teen's behavior rather than your own emotions.

51

2. Give clear instructions.

The purpose of this step is to tell your teen exactly what he or she needs to do to begin calming down. Give simple instructions like, *"Please go to your room or sit on the porch and calm down."* Or, you might make a calming statement like, *"Take a few deep breaths and try to settle down."*

As when you describe problem behavior, keep your words to a minimum. Don't give too many instructions or repeat them constantly; your teen could perceive this as lecturing or badgering. Simple, clear options keep the focus on having your teen regain self-control.

It is very important that you practice these first two steps. The emphasis is on using clear messages to help calm your teenager. Practicing this skill is time worth investing. Besides giving your teen important information about his or her behavior, clear messages help keep you on track.

3. Allow time to calm down.

This is the most important step in the whole process. If you remain calm, it's more likely your teenager will calm down faster. Simply saying, *"We both need a little time to calm down. I'll be back in a few minutes,"* can be very effective. Remember, giving your teen a little "space" helps him or her to "save face."

As you take time to calm down, you can think of what you're going to teach next. This "calm down" time also gives your teen a chance to make a decision – to continue behaving inappropriately or to begin calming down.

Come back to your teen as often as necessary. Ask questions like, *"Can we talk about what happened?"* or *"Are you calm enough to talk to me?"*

Move to *Follow-Up Teaching* only when your teen is able to answer you in a reasonably calm voice and is paying attention to what you say. You're not going to have the happiest child at this point, but it's important that he or she can talk without losing self-control again.

Take your time. Give descriptions and instructions as needed. Most of all, be calm and in control of what you say and do.

Part Two: Follow-Up Teaching

1. Describe what your teen could do differently next time.

Explain another way your child can express anger or frustration the next time he or she is upset. Kids have to learn that when they "blow up" every time something doesn't go their way, it leads to more negative consequences.

> **'Anyone who angers you conquers you.'**
>
> – Elizabeth Kenny

A good way to describe what your teen could do differently is to use an *"Instead of..."* phrase. For example, you could say, *"Instead of swearing, why don't you ask if you can sit on the porch until you are ready to talk about it."* Or you could say, *"Instead of slamming the door, please tell me you're mad and ask if you can go to your room to calm down."*

The purpose of this step is to teach kids what they can do the next time they get upset. You can teach your teenagers to recognize when they are beginning to get upset and when they need to ask for some time and space to regain self-control.

Once your teenager calms down, he or she can talk with you about the circumstances that triggered their anger. If parents and kids can learn how to talk about how they feel in these situations, they will be much more successful attacking the problem rather than attacking each other.

2. Have your teen practice what he or she can do next time.

Now that your teen knows what to do, it's important that he or she knows how to do it. By practicing, you are more likely to see the behavior you want the next time your teen starts to get upset.

A practice might sound like this:

Mother: *"Okay, Jamie. Show me what you'll say next time you're angry and you need some space."*

Jamie: *"Mom, I'm mad right now and I just need a few minutes by myself."*

Mother: *"Great! That's a great way to focus on calming down."*

After the practice is over, let your teen know what was done correctly and what needs improvement. Be as positive as possible, especially if he or she is making an honest effort to do what you ask.

3. Give a consequence.

This is a crucial part of *Teaching Self-Control* and something that many parents don't do. Some parents say they're so glad that their kid has stopped yelling that giving a consequence doesn't cross their minds. Others say they just don't have the heart to give a consequence because they don't want to upset their son or daughter any more than he or she already is. These feelings are understandable, but they don't help change a child's behavior. Consequences help change behavior.

An appropriate negative consequence teaches kids that they can't scream and yell just because things don't go their way. They can't use these behaviors in school without being held accountable. They can't use them on the job and stay employed. And most likely, they won't keep friends for very long if they can't control their tempers. As parents, we need to teach them how to respond in less harmful ways when they get upset. Consequences increase the effectiveness of your teaching, and the whole process of *Teaching Self-Control* helps kids learn better ways of behaving.

Putting It All Together

Let's take a look at an example of *Teaching Self-Control* with all the steps put together. Here's the situation: You have just told your 15-year-old son that he can't go to a friend's party this weekend because no adults will be there to supervise. He gets angry and begins cursing, then throws his gym bag across the room and breaks a lamp. *"You never let me do anything!"* he screams.

Part One: Calming Down

1. **Describe the problem behavior:** *"I know you're upset about missing the party, but you're yelling and swearing. "*

2. **Give clear instructions:** *"Please sit down on the couch and calm down."*

3. **Allow time to calm down:** (After allowing the boy a few minutes to settle down) *"Can we talk about this now?"*

Part Two: Follow-Up Teaching

1. **Describe what your child can do differently next time:** *"Instead of yelling and throwing things, let me know that you're getting angry and you need a few minutes by yourself."*

2. **Practice what your child can do next time:** *"Show me what you'd say if you felt like you were going to lose your temper."* (Boy practices appropriately.) *"Nice! Remember to use that next time you get angry."*

3. **Give a consequence:** *"For cursing, you lose phone privileges for two nights. And you'll have*

to use your lawn-cutting money to pay for the broken lamp."

Keys to Using Teaching Self-Control

Here are some key points to remember about using *Teaching Self-Control:*

Talk slowly and softly.

As we've discussed, a yelling match between you and your teenager does nothing to solve the conflict. In fact, yelling just makes the conflict worse. But if you can remember to talk slowly and softly as you speak with your teenager about your disagreement, you can make great strides toward toning down the conflict. Your soft voice tone also provides a model for your teenager for how he or she should respond to you.

Express concern and empathy.

When you're having an argument with your teenager, it's easy to let anger rule the way you respond. However, if you can express concern and empathy for your teenager, rather than giving free rein to your own anger, you will be in a better position to de-escalate the conflict between you.

Why? Because when you express concern and empathy, you force yourself to see your teenager's side of the conflict. And your expression of concern and empathy may help your teenager see that you've made an effort to meet him or her halfway, which might ease some anger on his or her part.

Avoid contact, and don't get sidetracked.

Avoiding contact means not letting physical touch, such as hitting, slapping, grabbing, or pushing become part of a discussion or argument between you and your teen. This only will make the situation worse and can significantly damage your relationship with your teenager.

Not getting sidetracked means not being drawn into an argument about issues that are not directly related to the conflict at hand.

For example, you and your teenage son are having a disagreement about his curfew time, and he says you are out of touch because all his friends' parents let his friends stay out until 1 a.m. If you reply by saying he doesn't know what he's talking about, that you most definitely are in touch with things, that you've always tried to be aware of what other parents are doing, and that you resent the fact that he thinks you are not caring enough to be in touch, then you have successfully been sidetracked by your son. He has diverted the argument from what his curfew should be to what curfew his friends have.

> **'Whatever is begun in anger ends in shame.'**
>
> – BENJAMIN FRANKLIN

In this example, you could reply to the boy's statement that all his friends are permitted to stay out until 1 a.m. with, *"You know, that's great for them, but we're talking about your curfew right now. Not theirs. And your curfew is midnight. What are some ways you can meet that curfew and still have fun with your friends who get to stay out later?"*

Be aware of efforts to divert you from the issue at hand, and teach your children to do the same in their discussions with others. Always focus on the main issue.

Control emotions.

As we've said before, it often is difficult not to let your emotions take over in a disagreement with your teenager. One way to stay calm is to focus on the *issue* at hand rather than your *reaction* to that issue.

Another suggestion is to be aware of the kinds of situations that trigger anger and other emotional reactions in you, and have a plan for maintaining self-control in those situations. Also, learn how your body responds when you're angry. Do you clench your fists or find that your neck tightens up? Do you get a knot in your stomach? Learn to read those signals and develop a self-control plan. Some self-control strategies include deep breathing, taking time away to cool down, muscle relaxation, writing or drawing in a journal, or positive self-talk, such as *"I can get myself under control."* These are also great strategies to teach your teenager to help him or her maintain self-control in emotional situations.

Have a "cool down" time.

If a disagreement with your teenager seems to be escalating rapidly, take some time away from each other. Having "cool down" time also models for teenagers a step they can take in a conflict they might have with a friend, teacher, or another person.

Summary

Parents must have a bountiful supply of patience if their teenagers have a problem with self-control. The wisest parents are those who realize that having their kids learn self-control is an ongoing process. It takes a long time. Don't try to rush the learning process; expecting too much too soon can create more problems than it solves. Be attentive to small accomplishments; praise even the smallest bit of progress your teenager makes. (And, while you're at it, give yourself a big pat on the back. *Teaching Self-Control* is a tough job.)

Look for small positive changes over time. Your teenager may have fewer angry outbursts, or the outbursts won't last as long, or they won't have nearly the intensity they once had.

Teaching Self-Control helps parents and their teenagers break the painful argument cycle. When tension is greatest in the family, *Teaching Self-Control* gives everyone a constructive way to get problems resolved.

So far, we have discussed *how* to teach our teens the values they need as they mature into adulthood. In the next few chapters, we will focus on *what* you should teach – the Six Pillars of Character.

TRUSTWORTHINESS

I will be as honest as I want my
children to be.

I won't lie to my children or in front of
them.

I will not treat honesty as a rule of
convenience by excusing acts of
dishonesty or deception as exceptions.

I will avoid hypocrisy like preaching against
smoking, drinking, or drugs while using
them.

I will demonstrate consistently the strength
of my moral convictions by paying
whatever price is necessary to do what I
think is right, risking loss of money,
approval, and even employment.

I will treat my word as my bond in all cases.

I will avoid legalistic escape hatches in
dealing with my children, honoring the
spirit as well as the letter of my
promises.

CHAPTER 7

Trustworthiness

The highest compact we can make with our fellow is –
"Let there be truth between us two forevermore."

– Ralph Waldo Emerson

Talk to a teenager about trust and you may get a deeply emotional response. Trust is a big deal for teenagers. Teen relationships are especially vulnerable to real and perceived betrayals of trust. Whether it's a friendship gone sour, a broken promise from a parent, or a failed romantic relationship, trust that's unraveled somehow never gets completely knit back together.

Trustworthiness is essential to meaningful and durable relationships. Everyone wants to be able to trust the people closest to them. Life is better and easier when it is full of mutual trust.

In fact, there are two sides to trust. One is *to trust,* to have faith and confidence in the intentions and actions of others, to believe that they will do the right thing. The

63

other is *to be trustworthy,* to demonstrate by words and acts that people can trust us. The first – whether we trust another – is a choice. The second – to be trustworthy – is an ethical obligation. Thus, people of character are worthy of trust.

The kinds of behavior that produce trust – integrity, honesty, reliability, promise-keeping, and loyalty – are called virtues, and every parent should try to instill these virtues in his or her children. This chapter is about helping your teen develop these virtues by teaching, enforcing, advocating and modeling them.

Teaching Trustworthiness

First, make a special effort to teach your teen to desire and value trust and the advantages that flow from being trusted. For example, a teen who earns a parent's trust will be given the benefit of the doubt in tough situations where what the teen tells the parent is contradicted by others or just seems implausible. Teens must understand that mutual trust is essential to meaningful intimate relationships, that untrustworthy behavior destroys relationships and that trust is an extremely valuable asset in the workforce. Finally, stress that it feels good to be trusted and awful to be distrusted.

Second, parents must teach teens what specific attitudes and behaviors produce and undermine trust. Trustworthiness is an unusually complicated idea that involves four major qualities: **integrity, honesty, reliability,** and **loyalty.**

Integrity

Integrity means moral wholeness as demonstrated by a consistency of thoughts, words, and deeds. (Often, this is described as "walking the walk.") But it is more than consistency. Integrity is frequently used as a synonym for good character because it involves strict adherence to a moral code.

Most young people value integrity quite highly but they don't always have a clear or accurate picture of what real integrity looks like. For some, integrity is simply "doing your own thing" or not being intimidated or influenced to do anything except follow their own impulses. Thus, some teens admire people they see as rebels even when those people are simply selfish or unwilling to control their passions.

It's not easy to teach integrity in a world that too often seems to confirm the cynic's credo, "Every man has his price." Youngsters see politicians, athletes, executives, and other adults abandon principles of right and decent behavior in order to keep their jobs or make more money. The task of parents is to put this dark side of reality into perspective and to give their teens a brighter vision of humanity and themselves. Teach them with words and examples that most people, most of the time, live good and decent lives despite constant temptations to do otherwise.

A primary task in teaching integrity is to shift the focus from the shortcomings of others to the demands and challenges of safeguarding one's own integrity. It isn't always clear where integrity comes from, but just about everyone has an inner sense of decency, a line he or she won't cross. The challenge for parents is to teach their children to draw that line at the borders of the Six Pillars of Character.

> '**I hope I shall possess firmness and virtue enough to maintain what I consider the most enviable of all titles, the character of an honest man.'**
>
> – GEORGE WASHINGTON

Teenagers should be receptive to discussions about integrity in part because most teens hate hypocrisy. They are often quite contemptuous of people who are insincere in efforts to flatter, appease, or curry favor with employers, teachers, or others who have authority.

When we were kids, we called it "kissing-up." The behavior was always regarded as shabby and fundamentally dishonest, and if you kissed up in the hope if gaining approval or advancement, you demeaned yourself. It is wise to teach your teen, however, that integrity does not preclude tact, respectful diplomacy, and sincere courtesy.

Prepare your teen for the fact that he or she will face many situations that require courage to resist temptations, to overcome pressures to abandon basic beliefs in order to please others, to get something they want a lot, or simply to stay out of trouble.

Moral courage is rooted in mental and emotional strength that allows us to live up to our highest values even in the face of criticism, possible embarrassment, and other undesirable results. Sometimes it's easier to risk injury than it is to risk being unpopular or losing something we really want, like a relationship or a spot on a baseball team or a part in a play. Thus, a good working definition of character is the *willingness to do the right thing even when it costs more than you want to pay.*

Another important aspect of moral courage is accepting what seems like failure or defeat without losing heart. Help your teen realize that disappointment and failure are unavoidable, that they are not fatal, and that even the most successful people fail more often than they succeed. In fact, many successes are built on the lessons we learn through failure.

While integrity asks us to courageously live in accordance with our inner beliefs, it does not prevent us from reassessing those beliefs and desires as we grow older and reorder our priorities.

Sometimes, teenagers think changing their minds means "selling out" some cherished belief or goal. Part of your job as a parent is to teach them that there is nothing shameful about thoughtfully abandoning goals in the face of new facts or conditions. Sometimes, we simply outgrow a dream. Learning when to let that dream go is an important part of growing up.

Honesty

The honesty aspect of the Pillar of Trustworthiness involves both what we say (our words) and what we do (our conduct). Honest people always try to convey the truth.

There are three aspects to honest communication: truthfulness, sincerity, and candor.

Truthfulness

Honest people are truthful. They do not intentionally misrepresent facts, intentions, or opinions. (We call this lying.) Intent is crucial to the distinction between truthfulness and truth. Being wrong is not the same thing as being a liar. An untruth told as the result of an honest mistake is not an act of dishonesty.

In teaching your teenagers the importance of honesty, they are bound to bring up situations where you lie or even where you want them to lie; for example, telling a caller you are not home or expressing joy over a gift that you really don't want.

You can't escape the fact that as important as honesty is, it sometimes gives way to other Pillars of Character like caring and respect. Even though it puts us on a slippery slope, we have to be honest with our kids: Not all lies are unethical.

There are times when an ethical person can be dishonest as a matter of kindness or respect. These well-intentioned lies are often called "white lies." Parents tell their children such lies frequently, whether it is about Santa Claus or the Tooth Fairy, or whether Barney is real. Saying you love an ugly gift or lying to a friend to get her to a surprise party fall into the same category. Only a fanatic would insist that we abandon all well-intentioned fantasy, surprise, humor, and kindness in the name of truthfulness.

But parents ought to give their teens guidelines that make it clear that all forms of dishonesty can potentially damage credibility and that good intentions are not always enough to justify a lie. They should teach their children to look at the lie from the perspective of the person being lied to. If that person learns of the lie, will he or she trust the liar less in the future? Will the person feel manipulated and betrayed or thank the person for caring?

For example, when kids eventually learn they were deceived about Santa Claus or the Tooth Fairy, they don't feel betrayed; their essential trust in their parents is not shaken. Children know the difference between stories and serious matters where reality counts. In the same way, most people happily forgive us for the small jokes and surprise-party deceptions. They are not likely to trust us less on other matters.

But some well-intentioned lies deprive people of important information they need in order to see their world more clearly. Consider, for example, parents of an adopted teen who lie about the facts of his birth, or a single mother who tells her daughter that her father is dead when he actually abandoned the family.

In these situations, the risk of broken trust is great. Remember this yourself and help your teenager understand that when people who have trusted us discover they've been lied to, it causes them to re-examine the whole relationship in the shadow of the question: *"What else have you lied to me about?"*

Sincerity

Honesty requires more than literal truthfulness. It requires sincerity, a genuineness of purpose that precludes all acts intended to create beliefs or impressions that are untrue, misleading, or deceptive, including deliberate omissions, half-truths, tricky word interpretations, and out-of-context statements. Parents should teach that it is as wrong to deceive as it is to lie.

Candor

Teenagers often have a particular problem understanding and dealing with the most advanced aspect of honesty, the obligation to volunteer needed information. This does not mean we have to volunteer everything we know or think (telling someone, *"Your hair looks awful,"* or *"I hate that sweater"*). We don't expect or want others to always give us their unsolicited opinions or foist upon us facts that could ruin positive feelings or assassinate other relationships.

But when we ask others to trust us, we assure them that they can rely on us to act on their behalf, to protect them. That is why trust relationships require us to be candid, sincere, and guileless. We are obliged to reveal things that those who trust us *ought* to know for their own good or *want* to know so that they can make informed decisions.

Reliability and Promise-Keeping

Teach your teenager that trustworthy people keep their word, honor their commitments, pay their debts, and return what they borrow.

Help them understand that commitments create ethical obligations and that they should always think in advance whether they are willing and likely to be able to keep a promise before they make it. Before they make a promise, they should think about what could happen that would make it difficult, undesirable, or impossible to keep their word.

Parents also must heed their own advice, especially in dealing with their children. It is very important when making a promise to be sure that your teenager understands what you are and are not promising.

People often hear what they want to hear, and it is human nature to interpret all ambiguous facts in a way that supports self-interest. So, if there is even a hint of misunderstanding, explicitly clarify what you understand your commitment to be.

It is common for teenagers to translate statements of possibility as promises.

"Will you get me a car if I get a B average?" your teenage son asks.

"We'll see, Billy. Just do your best," is your reply.

A month later, after getting a B average, Billy asks for the car saying, *"You promised."*

Of course, parents and other adults sometimes are deliberately ambiguous when they have no intention of doing what the teen wants. It is a dishonest ploy designed to buy some peace and quiet. Honesty requires that if we say that there is a chance of doing something, it is a sincere expression of willingness to do it under the conditions stated.

Cheating and Stealing

Cheating and stealing are two serious – but, sadly, all too common – violations of the Pillar of Trustworthiness.

A national survey conducted in 2000 by the Josephson Institute of Ethics showed that at least 70 percent of all high school students cheat at least once each year. About half admit to cheating repetitively.

Stealing likewise seems rampant. According to the survey, at least 40 percent of the males and 30 percent of the females admitted that they stole something from a store in the past 12 months. And about one in four high schoolers said they stole something from a parent or relative in the same period.

It's hard to believe that your kids would cheat or steal, but it is wise to accept the real possibility that culture puts great pressures on teens to sacrifice principles of honesty for personal gain and peer group approval.

Talk to your teens about the pressures they face. Let your son or daughter know that all people, including you, are in a constant struggle to live up to high standards of ethics and honor, and that the real measure of character is the ongoing commitment to self-improvement.

Loyalty

Loyalty – standing with and behind someone in need – is an important virtue. It is expressed in various forms of caring and respect. A good and loyal friend, for example, is physically and emotionally available to provide appreciation in times of triumph and support in times of trauma.

Loyalty is an important part of trusting relationships. Our loyalties are important signs of the kinds of persons we are. Teach your teen to choose carefully who and what they will be loyal to and then to take their loyalties seriously. Ignoring expectations of loyalty undermines trust and is interpreted as a betrayal.

Friends and relatives who demonstrate real pride and feel real satisfaction in the success of others prove themselves trustworthy. On the other hand, those who minimize accomplishments by indifference or belittlement, or who reveal even a tinge of jealousy, poison the soil where trust grows.

Another dimension of loyalty and caring is the willingness to give honest, constructive feedback. But timing is very important. Waiting to be asked is a good rule of thumb. Teach teens to remember that how they convey information often sends a louder message than the information itself.

Remember to reflect caring and respect in all your feedback. Parents and teenagers are often unnecessarily brutal and harsh in their criticisms of each other.

Familiarity does not justify tactless or unkind remarks. At the same time, a person who asks for an honest evaluation should be open to receiving it. It is discouraging when a person asks our opinion and then gets mad at us for giving it.

During moments of upheaval caused by tragedies and setbacks – a bad grade, being cut from a team, feeling rejected, a personal illness – there are opportunities to strengthen or weaken trust. Teach and show that loyalty is demonstrated by making time to be there, in person or by phone, by listening and actively trying to understand and empathize. Too often we feel we need to be able to say or do something that removes the pain when the most meaningful and eloquent testimony to our caring is just being there.

> **'Character is what you are in the dark.'**
>
> – Dwight L. Moody

But there are dangers in misunderstanding the obligations of loyalty or in elevating these obligations above others. Parents of teenagers should always be aware that young people can easily allow feelings of loyalty to friends and classmates to override their best ethical judgment.

Sometimes, the concept of loyalty may seem to demand lies, deceptions, and even illegal activity. Teach your teenager to choose their loyalties carefully because they can exact a high price. We should help teenagers realize they need to find ways to help and support their friends without sacrificing their own integrity and reputations. When loyalty demands dishonorable conduct, it demands too much.

Enforcing Trustworthiness

When a teen does anything that you consider to be untrustworthy, whether it is outright lying or cheating or more subtle forms of dishonesty, you should impose a consequence designed to send a clear message that this is not acceptable.

On the other hand, if your teenager demonstrates moral courage under pressure, be certain to praise the conduct.

Advocating Trustworthiness

Be certain your teenager knows that you want him or her to be a trustworthy person, that honesty is better than dishonesty, and that credibility and trust are great personal assets that can easily be destroyed.

Modeling Trustworthiness

H. Jackson Brown Jr. suggests that you should "Live so that when your children think of fairness and integrity, they think of you." Remember, you teach values not merely by what you say, but what you do.

Be self-conscious about demonstrating honesty, integrity, promise-keeping, and loyalty in all you do. Don't lie to save money or gain other advantages.

Don't lie or deceive in front of your teen or allow him to do so in front of you. Don't cheat on taxes or betray trusts. Avoid even petty acts of dishonesty that set a bad example.

Character in Action

After 15-year-old Tara baby-sat the toddler twins next door last night, their mother phoned Tara's parents to offer a compliment.

"Tara is so awesome!" the mother said. "She called me yesterday morning to let me know she'd be here at 7:30 and she came right on time. She also noticed that Jared seemed fussy when she put him to bed, so she made sure to tell me about that. The boys had a great time with her. We sure were impressed!"

Tara's father took the call and mentioned it to Tara later that day.

"Tara, I'm really proud of the way you handled that baby-sitting job. You called ahead and then you made sure you told the Cliffords about Jared being fussy. Sounds like you earned their trust. You'll probably be baby-sitting a lot with their kids."

Every day we have opportunities to praise our kids. In that praise, there often is an opportunity to talk about one of the Pillars. In the story, the father praised his daughter for being trustworthy.

The story shows how easy it is to use *Effective Praise* to encourage your teenager's positive behaviors. The father used the three steps of *Effective Praise* in just a few sentences. He **showed approval** by telling his daughter he was proud of her. He **described her positive behavior** by mentioning that she called ahead and told the parent about the fussy child. Then he **gave a reason** by letting her know she would probably get more work from the family because she was trustworthy.

The story also shows that you don't have to have long philosophical discussions about the Pillars to teach your kids how they fit into everyday life. In fact, taking an everyday situation, as this parent did, provides a valuable lesson in how important character is to what we do each day.

Thoughts About Trustworthiness

Here are some quotations that you can use to launch a discussion or make a point about trustworthiness:

- *Integrity is better than any career.*
  – RALPH WALDO EMERSON

- *What is right is right even if no one is doing it. What is wrong is wrong even if everyone is doing it.* – UNKNOWN

RESPECT

I will listen with respect and treat my
children's views seriously.

I will avoid selfish and petty behavior and
power plays, especially where my
children are concerned.

I will exercise self-restraint and maintain
the kind of self-discipline I expect from
my children with respect to violence,
yelling, or other displays of temper.

I will use only the kind of language I want
my children to use.

CHAPTER 8

Respect

People of character are respectful. But respect is not just a vital ethical virtue, it also is an essential foundation for good relationships. This is especially true of healthy parent-teen relationships.

Parents expect, and to a large extent, require their children to respect them both as individuals with feelings and needs and as authority figures responsible for the welfare of the family.

Teenagers who show disrespect by ignoring, belittling, insulting, cursing, or defying their parents make effective parenting difficult and unpleasant, maybe even impossible. Therefore, a central goal of good parenting is to teach children to respect their parents.

Parents, however, also have a duty to treat their children with respect. Again, this is not only a moral obligation but also a practical necessity for healthy relationships. Parents who yell, manipulate, insult, demean, abuse, or ignore their children erect huge barriers that impede effective parenting.

In general, treating people with respect means letting them know that their safety and happiness matter, and that their thoughts, wants, and needs are important simply because they are human beings.

Teaching Respect

If we want to teach our children to be respectful, we must translate the moral principle of respect into specific attitudes and actions. Here are seven basic rules of respect:

1. Honor the individual worth and dignity of others.

2. Treat others with courtesy, politeness, and civility.

3. Honor reasonable social standards of propriety and decency and personal beliefs, customs, and traditions that are important to others.

4. Treat others the way they would like to be treated.

5. Accept and tolerate individual differences and judge others on the content of their character and their abilities rather than religion, race, ethnicity, ideology, or similar factors.

6. Honor the right of adults and the desire of maturing children to control and direct their own lives.

7. Avoid using physical force or intimidation and refrain from improper threats of force.

We'll discuss each of these concepts.

Honor Individual Worth and Dignity

We should teach our children that the essence of respect is to show regard for the worth of all people and that the well being of all individuals is an important moral concern.

We should also teach them that people are not things to be used, manipulated, exploited, or taken advantage of for the pleasure or enrichment of others. Every single human being has value. Therefore, people of character treat all people with respect.

They also should develop self-respect so that they demand respect from others and refrain from conduct that is self-demeaning or self-destructive.

Children who are taught to note and appreciate the best qualities in others, to be generous, compassionate, and empathetic in judging, generally find it easier to respect people despite their faults. On the other hand, those that are raised in an atmosphere of fault finding and criticism and are taught to be cynical about human nature, are less likely to respect others, less likely to have heroes.

> 'I have decided to stick with love. Hate is too great a burden to bear.'
>
> – MARTIN LUTHER KING, JR.

But as your teenagers will quickly point out, some people – adults and kids alike – are "jerks." We can't demand that our children respect everyone they know. Esteem and admiration generally have to be earned. On the other hand, every human being, regardless of personal qualities, should be treated with respect, even people who do horrible things.

A powerful case can be made that some people – mass murderers, for example – relinquish any possible claim that they are *entitled* to be treated with respect. But even if that were true, it does not release us from our duty to treat such people respectfully. This duty is not based on *their* rights but on *our* responsibility to be better than they are.

During a political debate that began to sink to name-calling and mud-slinging, one candidate said, "Sir, I will treat you as a gentleman. Not because you are one, but because I am one." When we treat others disrespectfully, it damages our character.

We should treat others with respect not because of who they are or what they deserve but because of who we are and who we want to be. It is our own humanity, not theirs, that we affirm when we treat all people with respect.

Federico is 17 and his friends are making fun of him because he is still a virgin. They tell him it is an issue of manhood. Max, one of his buddies, says that his cousin Ellie is coming to town for a visit. He says that Ellie is a bit overweight and not very pretty but that she is "a sure thing." He says he will set up a date. Ellie suspects that the date is purely about sex and has no intention of having sex with Federico. But when he calls her, she agrees to the date, insisting that he take her to a very expensive concert and buy her an expensive dinner.

Federico and his friends were treating Ellie simply as a sex object, a way for Federico to lose his virginity. This is an extreme violation of the principle of respect. Ellie, however, was equally guilty. She intended to use Federico just as he wanted to use her. Neither she nor Federico were honoring individual worth or dignity.

Treat Others with Courtesy, Politeness, and Civility

We should teach our children to be courteous and polite, to say *"Please," "Thank you,"* and *"Excuse me"* not only to strangers and acquaintances, but also to family and friends. Courtesy and politeness are important social lubricants that reduce the friction of human relationships.

Respectful people are civil. They repress expressions of anger, disdain, and disappointment in deference to the feelings of others and the value of a peaceful and harmonious society.

Of course, there are times when a person must protest and speak out, but this can be done in a civil tone and a civil manner without insults, yelling, personal attacks, or threats.

The *way* one demonstrates respect varies from culture to culture, but the *obligation* to be respectful of the beliefs and traditions of others doesn't. So whether we shake hands, bow, or hug, we should greet people and part from them in a way that pays them respect.

If we know someone is likely to be offended by coarse language or certain types of humor, we ought to guard against giving offense. If we learn a person has particular dietary needs or religious beliefs, we should accommodate them when we reasonably can. In effect, we should go through life treating people as if they are our guests and we are their ideal hosts.

We should teach our children to treat their elders with more deference than they treat their friends. Perhaps the days of "Sir" or "Ma'am" are long gone, but surely we can still expect young people to use honorifics such as Mr., Mrs., or Ms., and to surrender a seat to an older person, a pregnant woman, or a person with a disability.

> **'Politeness is to human nature what warmth is to wax.'**
>
> – ARTHUR SCHOPENHAUER

We should also teach teens that courtesy and civility can improve their chances of getting what they want. People react positively to respectful behavior and negatively to rudeness.

In teaching respectful behavior to their teens, parents should remember that respect has to go both ways, or communication will break down. Teenagers often complain that they get no respect from their parents or other adults, that they hate being treated like they're still children instead of the young adults they are. They want to be listened to, and they want their opinions to be taken seriously. Teens often use the way they are treated to justify their own disrespectful conduct.

Parents should be more self-consciously respectful in the way they treat their children. Some adults treat kids with disrespect simply because they can do so and get away with it. Unfortunately, when we treat the powerless with disrespect, we not only reveal our own character defect but we also pass our bad traits on to the next generation.

Parents should be respectful of their teenagers' growing independence including everything from their musical tastes to their political ideologies. They must accept that their children are not merely extensions of themselves; they are separate, morally autonomous individuals.

Honor Reasonable Social Standards and Customs

Respectful people acknowledge the sensibilities of others. They honor reasonable social standards of propriety and decency as well as others' personal beliefs, traditions, and customs. This includes dressing, speaking, and acting in a manner that is not offensive. For example, it is disrespectful to go to church in short shorts and a halter top, to utter profanities to teachers, or to make ethnic or racial slurs or offensive sexual remarks.

Live by the Golden Rule

Respectful people follow the Golden Rule by treating others the way they would like to be treated. We don't want to be yelled at, insulted, or ignored, so we shouldn't yell at, insult, or ignore anyone else.

Both parents and their teenagers regularly violate the Golden Rule when it comes to how they communicate. They regularly signal disrespect through facial reactions, body posture, grunts, gestures, volume, and voice tone. Parents should teach and model communicating to their teen in such a way that if a neutral observer were watching the conversation between the two, he or she would know that both respected each other.

Parents and kids also have problems listening to each other. We need to remember that everyone wants to be heard. We should allow people to speak their minds, and we should listen to what they have to say. We can disagree with their opinions, but we should never demean their honest thoughts.

Another communication problem is nagging, which is essentially disrespectful. Yet many parents and children continually nag at each other. Respectful people are not meddlesome, rude, or offensive, nor do they demand that people agree with them or follow their advice.

The Golden Rule also gives us a framework to understand and deal with issues of privacy. Parents should teach their teens to recognize and honor other people's boundaries – the private places we're not allowed into without an invitation. Again, the issue comes back to consideration. Am I intruding? Could my inquisitiveness cause embarrassment, or even humiliation?

Teenagers seem to understand very quickly when their own privacy is being invaded, but have to be taught to recognize when they are trampling on the privacy of others.

Privacy issues pose a special problem for parents in dealing with their teenagers' sense of privacy. Can parents who suspect their son is taking drugs or that their daughter is having sex start searching for evidence in their teen's room or purse? In extreme cases, the answer may be yes, not because such an intrusion is not an inherently disrespectful invasion of privacy but because there may be no better way to advance the parents' right and obligation to look out for the teen's best long-term interests. In any event, such action is likely to be deeply resented and to seriously injure trust.

It might help to remember that the claim of privacy is not an absolute "right," especially where children are concerned. While it is not proper to intrude simply out of curiosity, when the stakes are high enough there are times when it is morally justified and legally proper for parents, teachers, and police to invade privacy in order to advance a greater good.

Accept Differences, Judge on Character and Ability

We should teach children to value and honor all people for themselves. Children of all ages, but teenagers in particular, can be cruel, insensitive, and exclusive toward peers who are "different" in some way.

We must teach our teens to listen respectfully to people with different ideas and backgrounds. This doesn't mean that we have to agree with other people or accept their opinions, but it does mean that we accept and tolerate their choices just as we ask them to tolerate ours.

Respect the Autonomy of Others

Respectful parents look for opportunities to give their children a meaningful say in decisions that affect them. By providing young people with the opportunity to participate in such decisions, parents show respect and teach responsibility.

This does not mean that the parent should give up the ultimate responsibility to make decisions affecting their minor children. It simply means that parents should begin as early as possible to train their children to be responsible.

Avoid Actual and Threatened Violence

Part of teaching respect to teens is training them how to resolve disagreements, respond to insults, and deal with anger peacefully and without violence. Respect for others also includes not using threats or physical force to get what you want or to express anger. Parents should teach their children how to deal with conflicts and disagreements through conversation and negotiation, and without using aggressive or violent behavior.

Respect is a very big concept to young people, especially in the gang sub-culture, which so strongly influences the attitudes and behavior of urban youth. In street jargon, respect means something very different than it does to moral philosophers. It is not something you owe others; it is something they owe you.

According to former gang member Nathan McCall, respect refers to a recognition by others that "I am someone to be reckoned with or someone to fear."

In gang-controlled neighborhoods, to "dis" someone – that is, to show disrespect, real or imagined – is a capital offense. If a person looks at a gang member in the wrong way, has the audacity to wear the colors of another gang in his presence, or simply dares to enter his 'hood, the conduct is treated as disrespect and the punishment can range from a beating to an assassination.

> **'Our patience will achieve more than our force.'**
>
> – EDMUND BURKE

This is a return to primitive, warlord brutality, where there is no caring, no regard for others, and no justice. There is no attempt to distinguish intentional acts from unintentional acts and guilty people from innocent ones. This, of course, is the antithesis of real respect.

Because this concept of respect-as-fear is prevalent in society, it is important to be sure that your children understand that real respect has nothing to do with fear. In fact, respect, like love, has value only when it is given freely and out of genuine feeling. Counterfeit expressions of respect generated by fear are really a form of contempt.

91

Parents need to understand that the likelihood of violent reactions can be reduced dramatically if teens are given specific strategies and techniques to help them develop and express self-respect in appropriate ways, to resolve conflicts and to solve problems without resorting to violence or disrespectful conduct.

Enforcing Respect

If your teen acts disrespectfully, point it out immediately and be ready to explain why the behavior was not considerate of the worth of others. Sometimes, that means teaching your teenager to be aware that what may be respectful in some circumstances may be entirely inappropriate in others.

But when your teen handles difficult people or circumstances respectfully and with a cool head, be sure you notice that as well, and praise him or her for it. Teens want to be thought of as mature, and nothing helps that more than when adults, especially their parents, acknowledge their "grown-up" behavior.

Advocating Respect

Let your teenager know that you expect him or her to recognize the worth of other people, whether he admires or likes them or not. Let your teen know that you expect him or her to show consideration for the rights, privacy, dignity, and property of others. And let your teen know that common courtesy and resolving disagreements nonviolently is not just good manners – it is simply a more practical way to live, making life better for everyone.

Modeling Respect

As with all training, teens need to see their parents model respectful behavior. You can show your kids how to be respectful in a variety of ways, such as:

- Listening to them without judging or criticizing.
- Letting them make their own decisions as much as possible.
- Not saying *"I told you so"* or gloating when the failure you warned about happens.
- Not making fun of them.
- Giving your full attention when they talk to you.
- Respecting their privacy and possessions.
- Using manners, avoiding negative comments and offensive language, and not arguing.

When teens see that they are treated with respect, it gives parents credibility and authority when they ask their teens to be respectful of others.

Character in Action

Andre sighed as he pulled on his jacket. "I remember when I actually liked going to work," he said to himself as he headed out the door to his job at the veterinarian's office. "Damn Dr. Lonergan! Why does he have to be such a bastard?"

For a couple of years now, Andre had worked part-time for Dr. Lonergan, a veterinarian and family friend. Andre had been excited to get the job. He enjoyed working with the animals and learning about their care.

But lately, Dr. Lonergan had been sullen and grouchy more often than not. In the past year, the clinic's business had grown tremendously. There were a lot of animals to care for. It seemed like Dr. Lonergan always was preoccupied. He didn't talk much to Andre or tell him what he needed done, but then got mad when Andre tried to take initiative and complete tasks himself. A couple of times, the doctor had yelled at Andre in front of the clinic secretary, Betty.

Andre didn't know what to do. He was thinking about quitting the job and finding something else, but he really enjoyed taking care of the dogs, cats, and birds in the clinic. He also needed the job to make his car payments.

Andre decided to ask his father, Farrell, what to do. He and his father were very close. "Two peas in a pod," Andre's mother often joked about them.

When Andre and Farrell talked about the problem, Farrell asked his son to explain the problem – how it began, Andre's feelings about it, and where it stood now.

After listening carefully, Farrell said, "The way I see it, Andre, there are a couple of key issues here. You and Dr. Lonergan need to communicate better so you can do your job. It's also important for you to stand up for yourself and not let him yell and scream at you, even if he is your boss. Maybe you should have a talk with him."

"But what would I say to him, Dad? Stop screaming at me?" Andre asked.

"Well, something like that, but in a nicer way. It sounds like Dr. Lonergan is overwhelmed with work and you could help him if he would just let you."

Farrell and Andre made a plan for Andre to ask Dr. Lonergan if he could sit down and talk to him about his work responsibilities. Before the meeting, Andre would make a list of jobs he thought needed to be done around the clinic and then ask the vet in what order the jobs should be done. Andre would tell the doctor that he thought he could help out more since they had gotten so busy.

Farrell and Andre practiced what the teenager would say to Dr. Lonergan so he would be ready. Farrell warned Andre that the doctor might be difficult to approach, but Andre should hang in there and speak up for himself.

> **'Fame is vapor, popularity an accident, riches take wings. Only one thing endures and that is character.'**
>
> – HORACE GREELEY

"Remember Andre, he's not a bad guy, just overwhelmed right now. He just needs a reminder that he should communicate better and that you deserve respect too," Farrell told his son.

Andre's low-key personality makes it difficult for him to stand up for himself, especially to an employer.

Self -respect – standing up for yourself appropriately – is an important character lesson for teenagers to learn.

Many teens like Andre are inexperienced in the ways of the world and may find themselves being trampled – emotionally or otherwise – by older, more experienced people. They may not know how to handle the situation and find themselves doing what Andre did – wishing the problem would go away instead of taking action to solve it.

Other teenagers may react differently. They may choose aggressive behaviors when challenged by someone like the doctor. They might quit the job, call the veterinarian a bunch of names, or even threaten him physically. The situation could become extremely volatile.

None of those ways is an appropriate solution to finding self-respect. Andre needs to work on being more assertive and asking for what he wants, while more aggressive teens need to work on asking for what they want rather than using physical force or threats to demand it.

Andre's father used *Preventive Teaching* to help his son focus on the Pillar of Respect to get his needs met. Farrell **described what his son needed to know** – the key issues involved with the vet not communicating and Andre's reluctance to speak up. Then Farrell **gave a reason** why communication and self-respect are important. Together, they **practiced** what Andre would say at a meeting with the employer.

Teenagers like Andre often need our help as they learn how to deal with "adult" issues like workplace conflict. *Preventive Teaching* gives parents a systematic way to teach teens these practical skills. Chapter 4 on *Preventive Teaching* has more detailed information about how to use this skill.

Thoughts About Respect

Here are some quotations you can use to launch a discussion or make a point about various aspects of respect:

■ *When evil men plot, good men must plan. When evil men burn and bomb, good men must build and bind. When evil men shout ugly words of hatred, good men must commit themselves to the glories of love.* – MARTIN LUTHER KING, JR.

■ *If you have some respect for people as they are, you can be more effective at helping them become better than they are.* – JOHN GARDNER, FOUNDER OF COMMON CAUSE

A PARENT'S PLEDGE

RESPONSIBILITY

I will demonstrate a willingness to admit when I am wrong and to take my medicine, and expect the same from my children.

I will avoid blame-shifting and excuse-making regarding my own shortcomings or mistakes and expect the same from my children.

I will assign reasonable age-appropriate responsibilities to my children and see that there are meaningful consequences if they fail to perform their duties.

I will insist that my children keep their commitments at home, school, and in extracurricular activities.

CHAPTER 9

Responsibility

Character is formed by doing the thing we are supposed to do, when it should be done, whether we feel like doing it or not.

— FATHER EDWARD FLANAGAN

Life is full of choices, choices as to what we say, what we do, and even what we think. And all our choices have consequences. Responsibility is an important aspect of good character that comprises the moral obligation to choose attitudes, words, and actions and the duty to accept personal responsibility for the consequences of those choices.

Teaching Responsibility

Responsibility is a complex virtue that involves 12 major concepts. The concepts are listed here and discussed on the following pages.

1. Being accountable
2. Exercising self-control

3. Planning and setting goals

4. Choosing positive attitudes

5. Doing one's duty

6. Being self-reliant

7. Pursuing excellence

8. Being proactive

9. Being persistent

10. Being reflective

11. Setting a good example

12. Being morally autonomous

Being Accountable

Responsible people are accountable for their choices; they accept moral responsibility for the consequences of their attitudes, words, and actions. Unaccountable people go to great lengths to avoid responsibility. They blame others, make excuses, and cover up.

Many young people are unaccountable. They often see themselves as innocent victims rather than material causes of the situations they find themselves in. Accountability requires reflection and analysis, and the ability to reconstruct events and locate the actions or inactions that contributed to a result. Parents can help teens discover the role their own actions and inactions play, see what choices they made, and understand how they could have made different choices.

Most teenagers want more personal freedom. They want more control over how they spend their time, where they go to school, who they hang out with, how late they can stay out, and whether or not they will have sex, drink alcohol, or take drugs. Yet many teens – and adults, for that matter – resist the responsibility that goes along with freedom. They prefer to blame their situations on others or on circumstances beyond their control.

Accountability is a major sign of moral maturity. Journalist Sydney Harris said, "We have not passed that subtle line between teenhood and adulthood until we move from the passive voice to the active voice – that is, until we have stopped saying, 'It got lost,' and say, 'I lost it.'"

Accountable people understand that both good or bad things will occur as a result of what they do and don't do, what they say and don't say, and what attitude they convey to others. The story below illustrates those aspects of accountability.

Sasha, a high school freshman, is invited to a football team party that will be attended mostly by seniors and even some college students. She is tremendously excited and her big question is what to wear. Her normal dress is fairly conservative but she likes to be stylish. She goes shopping with her friends Linda and Cindy. Linda says this is Sasha's chance, and that she should look "hot" if she wants to get noticed.

Linda picks out an outfit with a very short leather skirt and a skimpy top that exposes a bare stomach. She also suggests a radical hairdo and jewelry that suggests "wild." Sasha tries on the outfit and is amazed at how different she looks. She likes it. She is even considering getting a small temporary heart tattoo on her upper chest.

At home, Sasha shows the outfit to her older brother, Robert. "You look like a slut," he says unkindly. Sasha answers, "I look like the girls you take out. What's wrong with that?" Robert says, hypocritically and without irony, "You look like the girls I take out but wouldn't take home. Do what you want but if you want to be taken seriously, don't look cheap."

Robert suggests a much more moderate look. "But no one will even notice me," Sasha says.

What does a decision about what to wear have to do with responsibility? Well, what Sasha wears and how she carries herself might influence how she is treated and thought of, just as whether she accepts or turns down a beer or a joint at a party will affect the opinions others have about her and how they respond to her.

Since Sasha's choices will directly and dramatically affect how people react to her, she must be very clear about what reaction she wants. Often, teens get the response they want in the short term – lots of attention, a date, a feeling of being accepted – but are not aware of the price they may have to pay in the long run. If Robert is right, Sasha risks being labeled, disrespected, and not taken seriously. Sasha has to decide whether it is worth it.

While there is a scary part to responsibility, it is ultimately empowering to realize that the road to our future is paved by our own choices. Viewed this way, accountability is a source of power – and one very much needed by many young people who are thoroughly convinced that they have no control of their lives.

Exercising Self-Control

Ozzie is a 17-year-old basketball player with a hot temper. Although he is the team's highest scorer, he has been thrown out of one game and frequently talks back to the referees. Now his team is going into the championship playoffs. Ozzie's coach, worried about his player's lack of self-control, asks Ozzie to see Manny, a school counselor.

Manny: *"Well, do you think you will make it through the playoffs without getting into another fight?"*

Ozzie: *"Probably not. Someone will get me into a fight."*

Manny: *"But what if you knew that was the other team's plan: to take you out by getting you to lose your temper. Don't you see, it's not what the fight is about that's important; it's that they get you to fight. If you fight, they win and you lose. It's that simple."*

105

Ozzie: *"But you can't expect me to just take it when they push and elbow and talk trash at me."*

Manny: *"Do you think you prove your manhood by letting them pull your strings? Don't you see, if they can make you lose your temper, they own you."*

Ozzie: *"No one owns me!"*

Manny: *"Sure they do. Right now they are probably strategizing how to get you out of the game early. Don't you want to win?"*

Ozzie: *"Sure, I want to win, but what am I supposed to do?"*

Manny: *"First, remember that the only way you can win is not to fight. They are using your competitiveness and pride against you. You've got to treat it like any other game tactic. The issue is self-control. You have the power; you just have to decide to use it."*

Ozzie: *"How do I do that?"*

Manny: *"Play a little game with yourself. Don't treat the provocations as real acts of disrespect or anger. Treat them as tactics designed to gain control of you. Do you ever wonder how those guards with the big furry hats at Buckingham Palace in England are*

> *able to keep a straight face and stand
> at attention when everyone is trying to
> make them laugh or move? Well, they
> know that's their job. You can't score
> and help the team if you don't stay in
> the game, so a big part of your job is
> to resist any tactics designed to get
> you out of the game."*

Ozzie: *"So, you're telling me not to take it
personally?"*

Manny: *"That's right. It's just a tactic."*

Ozzie: *"I think I can handle that."*

Most teenagers want more control over their lives. Before this can happen, however, most parents want to know that their sons and daughters can control themselves, that they will think before they act, and that they will control their emotions rather than let their emotions control them. Responsible teens avoid dangerous or unwise impulsive behavior that is driven by anger or passion.

The mark of self-control is the ability to manage powerful passions and appetites (such as love, hatred, anger, greed, and fear) in honor of reason and moral duty. Responsible people don't use excuses like *"That's just the way I am"* because they realize that they are whatever they choose to be.

Teenagers can't always be expected to turn their feelings and emotions on and off. But we can teach teenagers that they can and should make conscious choices about how they express their feelings. People who can't control how they respond to their feelings are controlled by their feelings. In the case of teens, this can be chaotic, traumatic, and downright dangerous.

We can help teens make better decisions if we help them recognize the nature and source of emotions and teach them to harness these feelings so that they do not cause physical or emotional harm to themselves or others. Counseling teens through emotional crises is a vital parenting role, but this is an area where more than good advice is needed. Modeling is especially important. Parents who can't or won't control their own emotions can make things worse.

Parents should teach their teens that while the emotions and the feelings they generate are very real and significant, they need not dictate actions. **Taking charge of one's life begins with the ability to deal with emotions and moods in constructive ways through the exercise of reasoning and free will – the power to choose.** We should teach teens that no matter how helpless they feel in the face of their intense emotions, the power to choose is still there.

While it is natural to feel intense anger, for example, we should expect people of character to overcome the impulse to use violence. Similarly, we can understand that while people have powerful cravings – for unhealthy food, alcohol, cigarettes, etc. – they can refuse to indulge them.

It is essential that teenagers develop the judgment and discipline to avoid major blow-ups in the first place and to calm themselves down if they do "lose it." If that does not happen, the stakes can rise quickly. Out-of-control teenagers may harm others if their bad temper leads to physical violence. They may jeopardize a friendship with a torrent of angry words or get themselves into serious trouble with long-lasting ramifications.

Self-control is one of the most important lessons you will teach your son or daughter. It is nothing less than a survival skill, because people who cannot control their emotions have difficulty with every aspect of living in society, including having successful relationships with others and holding down a job.

Planning and Setting Goals

If you want to be successful, you first must identify what success means to you. Is it money, recognition, fulfillment, impact, personal happiness? Once you have identified what you want, you can set goals and make a plan to achieve them. Making a plan is a mark of responsibility.

Many teens resist planning. They would rather "play things by ear," confident that everything will work out. Parents have to help their teens develop the habit of setting and pursuing goals.

For teenagers in an overscheduled world, part of being a responsible person is being organized enough to manage time and to keep commitments and promises. Good intentions are not enough. Parents should teach their teens about planning and goal-setting to help them deal with the conflicting demands of school obligations, extracurricular activities, having a healthy social life, doing household chores and, in many cases, holding after-school jobs.

> **'You must have long-range goals to keep you from being frustrated by short-range failures.'**
>
> – CHARLES C. NOBLE

Writer Stephen Covey urges people to begin with the end in mind; people who plan live their lives more purposefully and are more likely to get what they want.

Helping kids prepare for the future is an important part of parenting, but it's difficult for several reasons. First, most teenagers tend to focus more on what happened today or what's happening this weekend than on planning for life after high school. It's hard to get them to think about the future.

Second, our daily lives can be so hectic that sometimes it's difficult to find time for long-range planning. But without that planning, we can't guarantee ourselves the kind of future we want. So we have to convince kids to make planning part of their lives.

This might involve some short-term planning exercises such as teaching kids to put gas in the car so they won't be stranded with an empty tank or run afoul of a parent who must try to get to work on fumes.

Long-term planning might involve lessons in career research or making sure high school classes and activities provide the right credentials for college. When you talk to your kids about long-term planning, your discussion also should include some information about how to set goals. The key to success in this area is to start early, well before urgent decisions are required. Here are some questions about planning that may help you and your teenager start making a long-term plan:

- Where do you want to go in life?
- What kind of person do you want to be?
- What kind of friendships do you want to have?
- What kind of job or career do you want to have?
- What things are really important to you?

To encourage short-term planning, teach kids to get in the habit of doing a mental inventory in preparation for an upcoming event. A good way to do this planning is by asking the who-what-when-where questions that define basic parameters. The basic questions teens can ask themselves might be:

- What do I need for this event (e.g, equipment and food for a camping trip)?
- What do I need to know for this event (how to get to the campsite, how to build a camp fire, how to put up the tent)?
- Who else needs information about the event (comparing supply lists with others going with me, letting my family know where I'll be and when I'll be home, getting time off from work or activities)?

- When is the event (making sure the trip doesn't conflict with another event that affects me or others; determining how the timing affects anything about the trip, such as the type of clothing I should bring; identifying things that must be done before the trip, such as applying for a camping permit)?

- Where is the event (how will I get there and back, travel time, etc.)

You can use some of the same inventory questions to teach teenagers how to do long-term planning, but kids need to know how to start the planning soon enough to fully benefit from it.

An important part of long-term planning is learning to set goals. Goal-setting may be a foreign concept to some teenagers because of their focus on the present. You can make setting goals seem more relevant to teenagers by explaining to them that goal-setting is a way to take control of a situation and hopefully shape it so things come out in their favor.

One way to teach teens about goal-setting is to have them write down goals they would like to achieve, then brainstorm the steps they think will have to be taken to achieve the goals.

Choosing Positive Attitudes

Viktor Frankl, survivor of a Nazi concentration camp during World War II, once said, "Everything can be taken from man except the last of the human freedoms, his ability to choose his attitude in any given set of circumstances...."

How we view the world around us affects nearly every aspect of our lives, including our physical and mental health and the relationships we have with others. Responsible people choose positive attitudes because responsible people accept control over their own emotions and, therefore, their happiness.

Positive or good attitudes such as trustfulness, optimism, cheerfulness, enthusiasm, hopefulness, and generosity produce better relationships and more productive work habits. Negative or bad attitudes such as cynicism, defeatism, suspiciousness, pessimism, hopelessness, and selfishness are all forms of prejudice that distort perceptions and often produce unwise and self-defeating choices. We do our children a great service by teaching and encouraging them to choose more positive attitudes.

Probably nothing does teenagers more harm than negative attitudes. The more these attitudes become entrenched in the personality of a teen, the more difficult they are to change. Thus, the earlier we can begin to encourage children to choose and nurture positive attitudes the better. The following story below is an example of how cynical and negative teens can be:

Tina is 15 years old and seems to be constantly angry. She wasn't always that way, but as she has gotten deeper into her teens, her sweet and pleasant disposition and her fun-loving nature have seemed to disappear. She is constantly at odds with her parents on everything: the way she dresses, the effort she puts into school work, whom she hangs out with, how much she talks on the phone, the way she talks to her parents, and the way she treats her younger sister. She doesn't want to do anything with the family and constantly puts down holidays and celebrations.

When her mother asks her where she is going, whom she is going out with, and when she will be back, Tina responds with sarcasm or an insult. She is becoming increasingly defiant. She is totally self-absorbed and takes everything personally. She tends to assume bad intentions in every act that affects her. She doesn't regard herself as pretty, and she is insecure about her peer relationships.

What specific attitudes can you identify that are driving Tina's life? What do you think are causing these negative attitudes? What positive attitudes would you like to see in their place?

Trying to teach teens to choose positive attitudes is difficult for at least four reasons: 1) Though they think they are open-minded, many teens have very rigid and narrow views on things; 2) Teens often think that the more intensely they feel they are right, the more likely it is that they are right; 3) Teen insecurities are easily transformed into anger or sarcasm; and 4) Many teens think that cynicism is a sign of maturity.

How can a parent teach a teenager to choose more positive attitudes? This is a tough assignment because the parent often is treated as the enemy. One option is to consider enlisting the assistance of other adults whom the teen admires or trusts to deliver the message. Perhaps it is an uncle, a teacher, a coach, or an older sibling.

> **'I discovered I always have choices, and sometimes it's only a choice of attitude.'**
>
> – Judith M. Knowlton

There are no sure-fire techniques to break through the walls that teens can build, but the right message, conveyed at the right time in the right way by the right person, can stimulate self-reflection, understanding, and resolve to change negative attitudes.

In this context, the parent must be opportunistic, looking for opportunities to communicate information and alternative perspectives in a non-accusatory manner, perhaps in reference to someone other than your own teen. And, parents must overcome their own negative attitudes and impulses. The challenge is to communicate in a way that will be truly heard and accepted. This means avoiding a self-righteous, accusatory, or "I told you so" tone or attitude. It is important to be a coach, to point out mistakes in a positive way with an eye toward correction and development, not punishment.

However they are communicated to teens, the following are messages that can stimulate attitudinal changes:

1. Attitudes are products of feelings. Always acting on feelings is unhealthy and unwise.

Teenagers sometimes think it is a matter of integrity to act on impulses. In fact, people of character recognize that impulses and urges may be natural, but they are not always pure or proper. It is as easy to want things that will improve our lives as it is to want things that might ruin them, but often the bad things seem more attractive. It's also important to teach our children that it is especially important to resist giving in to urges and impulses that could have long-term effects until there has been calm reflection.

2. While initial emotional responses of anger, sadness, and hopelessness may occur spontaneously, with reflection and willpower, it is possible to change one's perspective.

When we lose a competition, disappointment is a natural part of the process, but it need not turn into a lasting sense that we are losers. If we focus on what we did accomplish and the fun we had getting there, we can turn defeat into a learning experience.

3. How we react to an incident is determined by how we perceive facts and intentions, and our perceptions can often be based on erroneous assumptions produced by negative attitudes.

For example, if someone cuts in front of us on the road and speeds ahead, we are likely to feel angry (the root of road rage) because we assume the person was thoughtless or reckless. If we later discover they were rushing to the hospital with an injured child, our attitude would change completely. Similarly, if a boy doesn't call a girl for several weeks after a first date, many girls suffer feelings of rejection, even though there are many other possible explanations for him not calling: he lost her number, he's committed to someone else, or he's a jerk not worth wanting. When we don't really know why somebody did something, we are much better off with a positive, optimistic assumption than a negative one. In either case, we will sometimes be wrong, but we will live much happier lives if we give others the benefit of the doubt and presume people are innocent until proven guilty.

4. Accept what you cannot change.

The Christian theologian Reinhold Niebuhr wrote one of the most famous passages of wisdom about acceptance in what is called the *Serenity Prayer:* "God, grant me the serenity to accept the things I cannot change, the courage to change the things I can, and the wisdom to know the difference." Nothing is more futile and self-defeating than fretting over the things that cannot be changed. This includes certain things that have already happened (you were cut from the team, your boyfriend dumped you, your parents got divorced, a close friend died). To accept facts and move on does not signify a lack of respect for the event or suggest that powerful emotions associated with it are inappropriate. It is an affirmation of the future and a willingness to move beyond the past. Acceptance is also necessary when dealing with existing situations that you cannot change (your algebra teacher, the fact that you are less than five feet tall, your age). The sooner you accept these as realities, the sooner you can make whatever adjustments are necessary to live a happy life.

5. Selfishness is self-destructive.

Ultimately, selfishness separates us from others and prevents genuine intimacy. It is like locking our hearts in a dark dungeon. Preoccupation with "me, me, me" can lead to pleasurable moments, but never to a happy life. In addition, self-absorption causes youngsters to take things too personally by assuming that every act was done without regard for how it affects them. The message: *"It's not all about you."*

6. Bad things do happen, but the happiest and most successful people in life learn to put tragedies, failures, and hurt feelings behind them.

We should do everything we can to help our children develop resiliency – the ability to bounce back, to recover quickly, to get up after they fall down, and the capacity to learn from adversity and failure. Sometimes life is unfair; sometimes life stinks. But after appropriate commiseration, your message to your children, and yourself, should be: Get over it, suck it up, move on!

Doing One's Duty

Responsible people do their duty. They do what they are supposed to do when they are supposed to do it; they follow through on commitments and meet their moral and legal obligations. Doing one's duty is a hallmark of a person of character and a test of responsibility. Responsibility concerns the quality of character that causes us to accept both the notion of duty and a personal obligation to perform our duties.

As we have suggested before, no relationship contains more responsibility than the parent-teen relationship. Parents are not only responsible for their own lives, they are responsible to help their children develop the wisdom and character to live personally happy and socially constructive lives.

Being Self-Reliant

Responsible people manage their lives so they are not a burden or drain on others. To the extent they can, they pay their own way, provide for themselves, and are self-sufficient.

Generally, teenagers already see themselves as being self-reliant. They believe they can take care of themselves and make their own decisions. But, the reality is that teens are very reliant on their parents. For example, even when a teenager has a job and has money of his or her own, who pays for the house the teen lives in? The utilities he or she uses? The food served at the family table? The bed the teen sleeps in at night?

Still, parents have many opportunities to teach their teens to be self-reliant. We mentioned earlier about planning to avoid conflicts between classroom work and extracurricular activities and looking ahead to life beyond high school. Parents need to be involved in these matters, but they also need to make it very clear that the teen needs to manage these areas and not leave everything for mom and dad to solve or decide.

One of the goals of parenting is to teach children how to take care of themselves. Teaching self-reliance is a must, therefore, for successful parenting.

Pursuing Excellence

Responsible people strive toward excellence. They do their best, give a 100 percent effort, work hard, and are diligent. There is always a shortage of resources or time, but responsible people do the best they can with what they have, taking pride in whatever they do.

In a time when "whatever" seems to be the acceptable standard for everything, pursuing excellence certainly goes against the grain. And yet there is something truly special and personally rewarding about doing our very best work. Parents worry about their children's self-esteem and listen to all the latest "expert" methods for building it. But they often forget the tried-and-true method of pursuing excellence, which makes people feel good about themselves when they do a job well.

Parents should be supportive, encourage every effort, "cheer lead" when things aren't going well, and praise the positive results. The end product will be a teen who has genuine self-esteem and the self-confidence to take on the next task.

Being Proactive

Responsible people are proactive. They take the initiative to improve themselves, their conditions, and their communities. They seek to change systems and tackle social problems to make things better.

In his book, *The 7 Habits of Highly Effective People* (Fireside, 1990), Stephen Covey compares the difference between being proactive and being reactive to the difference between a thermostat and a thermometer. The thermostat *controls* the temperature. That's what it is designed for and that's what it does. But the thermometer only *responds* to what the temperature is.

Most of us spend our time reacting to life rather than being proactive in the areas we can control. This is particularly true of teenagers.

Think back again on the fictional examples of Ozzie and Tina. The one thing they had in common is that they reacted to circumstances around them rather than seeking ways to manage the things that were in their control.

One of the reasons teens respond this way is because they don't have the experience or the knowledge to understand that there are other options available to them. Parents have to point out what is within their teens' control and teach their teens to take the initiative to do what they can to improve their own situation.

Being Persistent

Another aspect of responsibility is persistence. Responsible people realize that all things worth doing are not easy; you often don't get what you want on the first try. They demonstrate perseverance and steadfast determination in pursuit of their goals. They stick to it and finish what they start.

Nothing discourages teenagers more than a lack of success. Take, for example, Carmen, a 13-year-old girl who has never played fast-pitch softball, but who tried out for her middle-school team. She's quite athletic but because the other girls have more experience at hitting and fielding, she did not do well at first. This is a small test of character. If she has developed the quality of persistence, she will practice until she gets better. If she sticks only with things that she is good at from the start, she will get discouraged and quit. Carmen could be one of the best players on the team if she develops her skills, but she has to be persistent.

If we help our children develop persistence, they become confident that they can succeed at anything they work at. This encourages them to take on new challenges. Life and individual growth demand it. Teenagers need to understand that in the beginning, mastering new skills is often difficult. There will be lots of mistakes, frustrations, and *seemingly* impossible obstacles to overcome. But persistence will pay off and competency will come and increase.

Parents have a special responsibility here to let children find their own limits and then encourage them to still push harder. Even when a parent thinks a teen is not suited for a particular activity that requires talent, such as music or baseball, persistence can pay off in improvement. And improvement is success.

In encouraging children to continue trying to master important tasks that are difficult at first, parents have to be ready for all the complaining, excuse-making, frustration, and even crying that will occur before mastery arrives. The reward is that once a task is completed successfully, the teen's confidence and problem-solving skills are increased so the next new challenge can be faced more easily.

> 'Energy and persistence alter all things.'
>
> – BENJAMIN FRANKLIN

One word of caution: There are times when it is appropriate to allow children to quit an activity they no longer enjoy. Sometimes, parents force their children to keep at an activity for their own personal reasons. A mother who always wanted to play the piano or a father who loves baseball may push her or his teen in those areas in ways that are essentially disrespectful and counterproductive.

Being Reflective

We've referred before to the interrelationship of the head, the heart, and habits. The responsibility to be reflective centers on "using one's head" to make reasoned and rational decisions.

Responsible people think ahead to anticipate the possible consequences of choices. They also think back about what they did and didn't do in order to obtain better understanding of a choice. Reflection also involves forcing oneself to think a problem through even when emotions and impulses are driving a person toward a spontaneous, thoughtless reaction.

Teenagers tend to think not just in the "now," but in the "right now": Will it be fun right now? Will it be easier right now? Will I enjoy it right now? They often don't think about the consequences, or, if they do, they think those consequences are so far removed from right now that it doesn't matter. But parents know that behaviors set into motion a chain reaction of events that not only affect the teenager, but other people as well. Reflection is the time spent examining what those chain reactions might be *before* acting out the desired behavior. We should teach our children to stop and think before they act and also to stop and reflect after they've acted.

> 'Self-reflection is the school of wisdom.'
>
> – Baltasar Gracian

One of the ways parents can help their children become reflective is simply by asking questions about the consequences of choices both before and after the fact. For example, *"If you don't go to summer school, how will you get enough credits to graduate?"* or *"When you decided to violate your curfew, what did you think would happen when you got home?"*

Whether you're speaking with your teens about sex, drugs, alcohol, smoking, or any other topic, ask what they think about the downside to those behaviors. If they say they don't know, give them information and ask for a response. Yes, you may end up in quite a discussion before it's over, with your teen seeming to take the opposite position of what you're saying. But stick to your guns, and you'll be surprised how often your teenager will walk away thinking, *"I never thought of that before."*

Setting a Good Example

Responsible people understand that their conduct often influences the values and behavior of others. They know they have a moral duty to behave in ways that promote good thoughts and conduct. Setting a good example involves two areas: leading by example and role modeling.

1. Leading by example

When an opportunity to do something meaningful presents itself, responsible people act. They don't make excuses. They take the initiative to do what needs to be done, even when no one else asks them to do it. And the response doesn't have to be some "great" thing either. Something as simple as holding the door open for a mother pushing a stroller or picking up the straws that someone else spilled on the floor of a fast-food restaurant are ways of leading by example. Parents have many opportunities each day to show

125

their children how to contribute to making life a little better for everyone.

Of course, some people may say that such "little" things don't really make a difference. But they do. Consider the story of an old man walking along a beach where thousands of starfish have been stranded by the tides. As he walks, he picks up starfish and throws them back into the water. A young man watches the old man do this, and as the old man nears, the young man says, *"There are so many starfish out here. You can't save them all. How can you possibly make a difference?"* The old man picked up another starfish and threw it into the ocean, and said, *"It makes a difference to that one."*

2. Role modeling

The story is told of a mother who was listening to her 18-month-old daughter play. The daughter was repeating sounds that she had learned. *"Moo, moo... cow. Meow, meow... cat. Woof, woof... dog. No! No! No!... Mama."* Young people – whether they're toddlers or teenagers – do pay attention to what parents say and do. That's why role modeling is so important.

Parents have to be aware that while lecturing and scolding may have their place, children will learn more about moral conduct and good character from the parental examples they observe daily. When parents tell their children to be honest and even impose consequences when they're dishonest, but then keep the extra change the store clerk mistakenly gives them, the message sent by the conduct is more likely to be what the youngster remembers.

"If Mom isn't really serious about honesty, then maybe she's not serious about other things," the teen might reason. *"Maybe Mom isn't serious about sex... or drugs... or drinking... or smoking... or stealing... etc."* Once a parent's credibility is destroyed, it is difficult to gain it back again.

An especially sensitive but extremely important area concerns the way parents handle their relationships. This includes their relationships with their own parents, siblings, spouses, former spouses, and, if they are single, their romantic and dating partners.

Single parents have a very special challenge and responsibility. Children's attitudes about dating, sex, fidelity, and intimacy are very strongly influenced by what they see their parents doing. Who the parent goes out with, how that parent behaves in every phase of the relationship, when and whom the parent brings home or introduces to his or her children, whether the person stays the night – all these things will be noted and in many cases replicated by the teen.

The point is simple: Parents can teach children all about the Six Pillars of Character, including explaining the words, their definitions, and the conduct they require. Parents can even establish household rules and consequences based on those Pillars. But if children don't see that their parents are serious about their own moral conduct, then the children may conform (because they have to), but their character development will suffer. So, parents, teach responsibility by being responsible.

Being Morally Autonomous

Responsible people think for themselves. They make independent, rational, ethical decisions based on an internalized sense of right and wrong (i.e., conscience) and they do not allow their attitudes and principles to be controlled by others.

Autonomy is a fancy word combining the ideas of self-determination, self-governance, personal freedom, and independence. Responsible people are morally autonomous because they think of themselves as free moral agents with the ability to reason and the freedom to choose right from wrong.

As youngsters grow, they may make difficult demands on parents, teachers, and school administrators. While empowering children with opportunities to state their opinions and voice their concerns on personal and family issues is a demonstration of respect as well as a good way for parents to teach responsibility, it is important to remember that families are not democracies. A teen's opinions should be respectfully heard and considered but they do not carry the weight of votes. Parental power should be exercised with wisdom, sensitivity, and expertise; it should not be abdicated.

Letting your children outvote you on subjects such as where you live, what schools they go to, and whether they go to their piano lessons or go to Grandma's house for dinner is not so much a demonstration of respect as a relinquishment of the leadership prerogatives that is part of the job of parenting.

As children get older, more and more independence should be granted. And without compromising important family values and financial resources, children should have a significant voice and, eventually, broad autonomy in areas such as their clothing, hairstyle, room decoration, book and music selection, friends, and extracurricular activities. Yet even in these areas, a caring, responsible parent may properly exercise control in the best interests of the teen.

Teaching teens to be morally autonomous – to make their own decisions based on their own values – can be difficult. Despite fierce desires to be thought of as unique individuals, teens have a historic tendency toward conformity and a susceptibility to peer pressure. Thus, youngsters tend to think and act as their friends do. We can see this in the way teens dress and talk. We can see it in the music they like and the people they think are cool and uncool. It even shows in the way they treat other people. Exclusionary cliques, teasing, taunting, and bullying are usually group activities. It's as if teens want to be unique without being really different.

> 'I long to accomplish a great and noble task, but it is my chief duty to accomplish small tasks as if they were great and noble.'
>
> – HELEN KELLER

This is why your children's choice of friends is so vital. If they hang out with kids who smoke, use drugs or alcohol, drive recklessly, or engage in casual sex, the likelihood is high that your teen will engage in similar conduct. The mantra *"But all my friends are doing it"* is every parent's nightmare.

A teenager has to be taught that even though "all my friends are doing it," he or she is still a person who makes his or her own choices. Someone once said that right is still right even if no one else is doing it, and wrong is still wrong even if everyone else is doing it. Teenagers have to be given character training, which gives them the courage to go against the crowd and be responsible to their own beliefs and convictions.

Identifying and Labeling Choices

Be sure you teach your teens that their attitudes, words, and actions are a matter of choice and that they will be held responsible for the consequences of their choices.

When things are not going the way teenagers want them to, one of the most valuable things parents can do is to help them identify the choices they made that contributed to the current situation. Help them understand how those choices set into motion factors that created the situation they now must deal with.

It is especially important to stress over and over again that teens have more power than they realize, even over the attitudes and behavior of others. The way the teenager approaches a problem, the tone of voice, body posture, timing – all these things influence reactions.

Enforcing Responsibility

While we've put special attention on self-control because that is such a major issue for so many teens, all aspects of responsibility are important. The responsibility of the parent in teaching responsibility is to be sure that teenagers experience appropriate positive and negative consequences for their choices. We'll talk more about consequences in the "Character in Action" section in this chapter.

By all means, praise the teen who demonstrates accountability, persistence, self-reliance, and other hallmarks of responsibility. But also be sure that verbal reactions and other actions demonstrate your seriousness about these matters.

Advocating Responsibility

Be certain your teenager knows the high value you place on responsibility in all its aspects: accountability, self-control, pursuit of excellence, choosing positive attitudes, thinking ahead, and persistence.

Modeling Responsibility

The best way to teach responsibility is to be responsible yourself. Monitor your own behavior very carefully.

Be visibly and openly accountable for your choices, especially your mistakes. Don't blame others or make excuses. Be sure that you are demonstrating self-control over your own emotions and impulses and that you consistently demonstrate the positive attitudes you want to see in your teen. In the next section in this chapter, we'll talk more about the qualities of a responsible parent.

Character in Action

Amanda knew she shouldn't have lied to her parents about going to the party with her friends. She told her parents she was going to the movie with Craig, but instead she and Craig went to a party at the fraternity house where Craig's brother lived.

It was a cool party. Everyone was in college, not high school like Amanda and Craig. They drank some beer, but not a lot, and talked to some of the guys who lived in the fraternity with Craig's brother. Craig said he wanted to try and get into that fraternity in two years when he finished high school. Amanda wasn't sure about joining a sorority, but the girls from the sorority she talked to at the party seemed nice.

It was midnight when Craig took Amanda home, and she congratulated herself for making her curfew and getting away with the lie. She felt a little irresponsible about it, but told herself that sometimes you just have to be a little rebellious.

The next morning, when her mother, Toni, asked, "How was the movie?" Amanda said, "Just okay. Not great."

"Which one did you see?" Toni asked.

"Oh, it was an action one. I can't really remember the title," Amanda said, knowing that she was very close to being found out.

Toni looked intently at her daughter. "You didn't go to the movie did you, Amanda?"

"Damn!" Amanda thought. "Why did Mom have to be so smart?"

"No, Mom. We went to a party up at the college," Amanda said quietly.

"I know," Toni said. "I called the theater last night. My friend Trudy was working and she said she didn't see you and Craig come in. Why did you say you were going to the movie?"

"Because I knew you wouldn't let me go to a college party."

"You're right. I don't think you're old enough for that, and even though I like Craig very much, I don't think he's old enough either. You're grounded for the next two weekends."

Amanda couldn't believe it. "Two weekends! It wasn't that big a deal, Mom."

"Yes it was, Amanda. You lied to us, and you went to that party knowing it's not something we would have approved," said Toni.

"But it's like you don't respect me at all. I can't make any decisions without you questioning them!" Amanda cried.

"Amanda, I want you to learn about making good decisions, but when you made a choice to go to that party, you showed me that you don't respect our family rule – always let someone know where you are. When you made that decision, you showed me that you are not responsible enough to make the right decision. I'm disappointed in you. You may think I'm just being mean by grounding you, but you earned this consequence by making a bad choice. I care about you. I want you to learn to be responsible."

As the parent of a teenager, you may have mixed feelings about checking on your child's whereabouts. You want him or her to be able to take responsibility and make good decisions, but you know that immaturity and peer pressure can be powerful and that teens won't always make good choices. That's why you should always know what your kids are doing, even if that means doing some detective work. Remember, you're a parent, not a friend.

But how do you check on your kids? Some parents have this standing rule: "If you ask me to go somewhere, be prepared to tell me where you're going, who you're going with, and who will be there. Also, let me know what you're going to do, how long you'll be there, how you will get there and get back home, and what time you'll arrive home."

It seems like a lot of questions, but don't be afraid to ask them all and any others that occur to you. After all, you have ultimate responsibility for the young person standing in front of you, even if he or she is nearly grown and whines every time you ask, *"Where are you going?"*

The bottom line is, don't be afraid to check on your kids, and let them know that you *will* check. Then do it. Make a call if something doesn't seem right. Now, we're not saying that you check every time or follow your son or daughter. It's more a matter of communicating to your kids that you'll be doing your job as a parent and they need to be responsible and trustworthy about their behaviors. They may wail that you don't trust them, but remember, trust is earned.

Don't worry about being the only parent who checks on his or her kids. You're not! If you have developed a good relationship with your kids, you'll already have a great deal of information about the friends who are important to them and the places they like to go. This will give you basic foundational information about most of their activities.

And tell your teens that they can use you as a great excuse for not joining in an activity that they feel uncomfortable with or feel is inappropriate. *"My parents would ground me for six months!"* is a viable excuse in those circumstances, and it may let your son or daughter escape a situation without feeling like a coward.

Using Consequences

At Girls and Boys Town, using consequences is an important part of teaching because it helps kids make a connection between what they do and what happens to them afterwards. It's an integral part of learning to be responsible.

As you think about what consequences you will use with your teenager, remember that you must first establish clear expectations for behavior and how failure to meet those expectations triggers consequences.

Kids need to know, for example, that their curfew is 9 p.m. on school nights and 11 p.m. on weekends (or whatever time you decide), and that those times were chosen to make sure they get enough sleep and for safety reasons. Kids also need to know the consequences for violating their curfew.

Talk with your kids about your expectations, the rationales behind your expectations, and how those expectations relate to consequences. Make sure they understand that their behavior will result in a consequence.

Make sure you are consistent about issuing consequences. Don't let something go one time and issue a heavy consequence the next time the same behavior occurs. That inconsistency just tells your kids that they might as well test your limits, because they may catch you on a lazy day and not get a consequence.

Consequences are most successful when they relate to the expectation the teenager failed to meet, such as withdrawing driving privileges for a youth who fails to put gas in the car.

You can use different kinds of consequences with teenagers. Generally, the smaller the consequence, the better. When consequences are too big, they take the focus off the inappropriate behavior.

Removing privileges, such as not letting your teenager drive the car, is one type of consequence. You also may use short-term or long-term consequences. Short-term consequences might be assigning chores such as doing the dinner dishes. Long-term consequences might involve grounding or a loss of some type of privilege such as using the telephone.

Keep the acronym SANE in mind as you develop consequences for your kids:

Small consequences are better.

Avoid punishing yourself with the restrictions you place on your child (e.g., restricting a teen's use of a vehicle so that you have to drive him or her everywhere for several weeks).

Never abuse your child with a consequence.

Effective consequences are consistent consequences.

Consequences help teach kids about the cause-effect relationship between what they do and what happens because of their actions. Many times, as we talk to our kids about consequences, we encourage them to make good choices about their behavior by telling them that good things are more likely to happen to them if they behave well. But we all know that sometimes that doesn't hold true. Sometimes, the kid who cheats on the test gets away with it, and the kid who returns the lost wallet is jeered by his friends. When kids see things like this, they wonder what benefits there are in choosing moral behaviors. They may begin to focus on "getting by" with things and not getting caught, rather than on doing what's right.

As parents, we need to continue to reinforce positive values and give negative consequences for bad choices. Our kids need to believe that it's important to know what the right thing is, and to try to do it because it's the right thing – the moral and ethical thing – to do.

One father we know taught his son and daughter that they were obliged to make moral choices because those choices were the only true measure of the worth of a man or woman. Nothing else mattered, he told his kids. *"After everybody else goes home,"* the father said, *"you still have to live with yourself."*

Thoughts About Responsibility

Here are some quotations you can use to launch a discussion or make a point about various aspects of responsibility:

Accountability

■ *Parents can only give good advice or put them on the right paths, but the final forming of a person's character lies in their own hands.*
  – ANNE FRANK

■ *Though we have no choice about what happens to us, we always choose what happens in us.*
  – MICHAEL JOSEPHSON

Self-Control

■ *An event triggers a process of responses that can often be filtered or controlled by the mind before it reaches the heart, stomach, and muscles.*
  – UNKNOWN

Positive Attitude

■ *You accept things as they are, not as you wish they were in this moment... The past is history, the future is a mystery, and this moment is a gift. That is why this moment is called the present.*
  – DEEPAK CHOPRA

- *If you change your mind, you can change your life.* – WILLIAM JAMES

Duty

- *Without duty, life is soft and boneless.*
  – JOSEPH JOUBERT

- *Duty is the sublimest word in our language. Do your duty in all things. You cannot do more. You should never wish to do less.* – ROBERT E. LEE

Being Proactive/Taking the Initiative

- *To ignore evil is to become an accomplice to it.*
  – MARTIN LUTHER KING, JR.

- *Where there's a will there is a way. Where there's not, there's an alibi.* – ANONYMOUS

Planning and Setting Goals

- *True happiness… is not attained through self-gratification, but through fidelity to a worthy purpose.* – HELEN KELLER

- *Begin with the end in mind.* – STEPHEN COVEY

Being Persistent

- *Sure I am of this, that you have only to endure to conquer. You have only to persevere to save yourselves.* – SIR WINSTON CHURCHILL

- *Patience and tenacity of purpose are worth more than twice their weight of cleverness.*
  – THOMAS HENRY HUXLEY

Being Reflective

- *He who never sacrificed a present to a future good, or a personal to a general one, can speak of happiness only as the blind speak of color.*
  – HORACE MANN

- *Think all you speak, but speak not all you think. Thoughts are your own; your words are so no more.* – PATRICK DELANY

Setting a Good Example

- *We don't choose to be role models, we are chosen. Our only choice is whether to be a good role model or a bad one.* – KARL "THE MAILMAN" MALONE, PROFESSIONAL BASKETBALL PLAYER

Being Morally Autonomous

- *Either you think – or else others have to think for you and take power from you, pervert and discipline your natural tastes, civilize and sterilize you.* – F. SCOTT FITZGERALD

- *When you have to make a choice and don't make it, that in itself is a choice.* – WILLIAM JAMES

FAIRNESS

I will not resort to arbitrary power to get
my way when I have taught that
general rules of fairness are applicable.

I will treat all my children, including my
stepchildren, equally and fairly.

I will be open and reasonable to discussion
and criticism.

CHAPTER 10

Fairness

All virtue is summed up in dealing justly.

– ARISTOTLE

How old were you when you first learned that the world isn't fair? Most of us felt the sting of unfairness very early in life. Perhaps you were blamed for something you didn't do or were excluded from a club or team just because someone didn't like you. Perhaps you were given a lower grade than you deserved because the teacher had it in for you. And, at one time or another, you probably experienced the frustration of not being able to fully explain your side of the story. That few of us escape these everyday inequities doesn't make them hurt less.

Many people also have experienced the outrage of racial, religious, or gender prejudice. We learned early on that life isn't always fair or rational. And we know by now that that fact doesn't necessarily change as we become adults.

Children seem to grasp the concept of fairness at a gut level. If you don't believe that, just listen to them playing together. It won't take very long until one of them says, *"That's not fair!"* They understand that someone has broken a rule, or made a decision, or behaved in such a way that has put them at a disadvantage, and it's not "fair."

Parents are also aware that teenagers have their own sense of what's fair. It seems like almost anytime a parent makes a decision denying a teenager something he or she wants, the parent is going to hear the same refrain, *"It's not fair!"*

Well, what is fair?

As it happens, what is or is not fair turns out to be much more complicated and ambiguous than it seems from the vantage point of the person who feels short-changed. While the underlying concepts of fairness and justice are simple, almost intuitive, applying them in real life proves to be a very difficult task. As Ralph Waldo Emerson said, "One man's justice is another's injustice."

Teaching Fairness

We should teach our children that fairness is concerned with actions, consequences, and processes that are consistent with moral rightness and are honorable and equitable. Fair decisions are made in an appropriate manner based on appropriate criteria.

Fairness is closely related to the concept of justice. We are more likely to think and speak in terms of the word "justice" when we are dealing with broader social issues and institutional obligations to individuals. We are more likely to use "fairness" in the setting of everyday interpersonal relationships.

Our devotion to justice is deeply ingrained. Aristotle said that "All virtue is summed up in dealing justly," and the concept is so central to civilized governance that in 1215, the Magna Carta provided: "to none will we... deny or delay right or justice." This reverence for justice is evident in all of America's founding documents and, on a regular basis, Americans pledge allegiance to a Republic that stands for "liberty and justice for all."

> 'One thing people cannot bear is a sense of injustice. Poverty, cold, even hunger, are more bearable than injustice.'
>
> – MILLICENT FENWICK

Even Superman's motto, "truth, justice and the American way," reveals the unbreakable linkage between the pursuit of justice and our national identity. Not surprisingly, we take very seriously the obligation to do justice and rectify injustice as best we can.

You can be sure that your teenager has been exposed to at least some of these notions of justice and feels entitled to just and fair treatment. Parents must respond to their children's desire to be treated fairly but also must teach them of their duty to be fair and play fair.

But fairness is also central to the parenting role itself. Parents have a great deal of control over the lives of their children. They can assign chores, give criticism and praise, give gifts and dole out punishments, and if they have several children, there is always an issue of consistency. With this power comes the responsibility to be fair.

There are two aspects to being fair: *fair results* (substantive fairness) and *fair procedures* (procedural fairness).

Substantive Fairness

A fair result generally is one in which people are given what they are due, what they deserve. The problem is that there is no agreed-to standard for determining what a person "deserves."

Take, for example, the basic question of taxation. What is a fair allocation of burdens? Some argue that the true measure of fairness is equality – every person should pay the same flat tax. Others believe that tax rates should be based on income so that those who earn more pay more; this is called a progressive tax. While the results under each theory are dramatically different, both positions are justifiable from the perspective of fairness.

The wide variety of approaches to the question "What is fair?" means that no matter what decision is made, someone can claim the result is unfair. And they're right – at least according to their personal criteria. Thus, it is often not possible to come to an indisputably fair result.

One of the things that parents have to deal with is that even when they make decisions according to the known rules of the family, disagreements and criticism – including charges of unfairness – from their teens are inevitable. When your teens consider themselves "winners" (i.e., they get what they want), they will think your decision is just. But when they think they "lost" (i.e., they didn't get what they want) they will consider that decision as unjust. That just comes with the territory of being a decision-maker, and all parents can do is their very best to reach a fair judgment based on personal conscience and ethically justified standards of fairness.

Procedural Fairness

How one goes about reaching a decision is another crucial aspect of fairness. Important decisions should be made carefully, honestly, and objectively. Simply put, fair decisions are made in an appropriate manner based on appropriate criteria.

Whatever procedure parents use to make decisions that affect their teens has to be open, careful, honest, and objective. Suppose, for example, that you found a marijuana cigarette in the room of your 15-year-old daughter, Jenna. Jenna claims she knows nothing about the joint. She says it might be Lydia's (a friend who comes over a lot) or that maybe it was planted by her older brother to get her in trouble. Both Lydia and her older brother deny they had anything to do with it.

Before you decide whether to impose any form of punishment on Jenna, you should review these four essential elements of procedural fairness:

1. Fair notice

Does Jenna know your rule or expectations regarding marijuana? Does she have any idea of what her punishment might be if she violates those expectations?

2. Impartiality

Be sure you are analyzing the situation and charges objectively without a bias.

3. Gather facts

Find out whatever information you can, including checking out Jenna's theories on what happened

4. Fair hearing

Be sure to give Jenna a fair and full opportunity to explain her side of the story. As she explains her actions, you should try to listen carefully with an open mind. Thoroughly investigate until you're satisfied that everything important has been brought up and that you understand the situation. If you need to call other teens or their parents to confirm the information your teen gave, try to do so without causing undo embarrassment.

> **'Justice is conscience, not a personal conscience but the conscience of the whole of humanity.'**
>
> – ALEXANDER SOLZHENITSYN

This opportunity to explain and defend herself is very important to your teen and to being fair in deciding what may need to be done about the rule violation. After all, what is worse than being accused of doing something without being given the chance to stand up for yourself?

The next step that should follow a fair procedure is a fair decision – one where your teen receives what he or she is due or deserves according to the circumstances. Simply put, that means that any consequences or punishment should match the offense.

Let's suppose that your son comes home at 12:30 a.m., an hour past his curfew. You ask him what happened, and he explains. After you are sure you have all the details, it becomes clear to you that he really has no excuse for being late; he was simply negligent about keeping track of the time. So then you ground him for a year, right?

While you may be tempted to do that because of all the worry he caused you and the irresponsibility he displayed, grounding him for a year is hardly a fair punishment for the offense he's committed. Grounding him for the next weekend would be a more reasonable and fair consequence for breaking the curfew.

Enforcing Fairness

Use positive and negative consequences to reinforce your teenager's ability to be fair. Offer praise for a teen's positive use of fairness. Impose a negative consequence for actions your teenager takes that aren't fair.

Advocating Fairness

Make sure your teenager knows that you expect fairness from him or her as much as he or she wants fairness from you. If your teen wants a fair application of rules, he or she should also be willing to put forth the effort to follow the rules and not try to squeak by with minimum effort.

Modeling Fairness

Modeling fairness is really what this chapter has been about. Since applying the rules of fairness is not always easy or clear, it is vitally important that your teen sees you making the effort to be as open, honest, and objective as you can be in reaching decisions.

Character in Action

Fourteen-year-old Lenny was so excited! His lawn-cutting business was just getting off the ground, and today he earned his first big paycheck! Mrs. Crandall, the elderly lady next door, paid him $40 for cutting her lawn.

Lenny ran home to show his father. "Dad! I got $40 for doing Mrs. Crandall's lawn!"

Lenny's father was amazed.

"Lenny, let's talk about this for a minute. Look at Mrs. Crandall's yard. How big would you say it is?"

Lenny glanced at the tiny yard. "It's pretty small. It only took me about 20 minutes to cut it."

"So you got $40 for 20 minutes' work, right? Do you think that's fair to Mrs. Crandall?"

"Well, she's pretty old. I doubt if she could cut it herself, so I'm helping her out by cutting it."

"That's right, you are helping. But if it was your yard, would you pay $40 to have it cut?"

"No way!"

"How much would you pay?"

Lenny looked at his father. He knew now what his father was getting at. He needed to return some of the money to Mrs. Crandall.

"I guess it's worth about $20 or $25," Lenny said. "I'll return some of the money to her."

"That's good, Lenny. I know it's hard to give the money back, but it's the fair thing to do. Mrs. Crandall is almost 90, and she's used to her nephew cutting the lawn for free. You know, if you charge her a fair price for the work you do, she's more likely to ask you to cut her yard again. You may have a steady customer!"

"I know, Dad. I'll go over after lunch and talk to her."

Lenny's father used *Guided Self-Correction* to help his son see what was unfair with his behavior.

The father used a series of questions to get Lenny to see the problem, rather than just telling him to return the money. By answering the questions, Lenny used some rational thinking skills to figure out what was wrong and find a way to be fair with Mrs. Crandall.

Near the end of the teaching, the father used **praise and empathy.** Lenny's father said, *"That's good, Lenny. I know it's hard to give the money back, but it's the fair thing to do."* With his combined praise and empathy statement, Lenny's father let him know that he approved of Lenny's plan to return the money and he showed his son that he knew it was a difficult thing to do.

The father also tried to help Lenny see how doing the right thing – being fair – might benefit Lenny in the long run, by earning him Mrs. Crandall's loyalty, Lenny had a better chance of getting a steady lawn-cutting job.

Thoughts About Fairness

Here are some quotations you can use to launch a discussion or make a point about various aspects of fairness:

- *Injustice is relatively easy to bear; what stings is justice.* – H. L. MENCKEN

- *In America people never obey people, they obey justice, or the law.* – ALEXIS DE TOCQUEVILLE

CARING

I will remember my children are
stakeholders in everything I do.

I will demonstrate compassion and respect
for others, especially my children.

I will be visibly charitable and involve my
children in choosing charities to
support.

I will not discount, belittle, or trivialize my
children's feelings and fears.

CHAPTER 11

Caring

> "Life's most persistent and urgent question is,
> 'What are you doing for others?'"
>
> – MARTIN LUTHER KING JR.

Sometimes, it's very easy to be selfish. It is easy to get so caught up in our daily activities and responsibilities that we don't take the time to think about and attend to the needs of others, even those in our own families. In fact, we tend to take the people closest to us for granted.

It is natural for teenagers to be self-absorbed. They are still learning about themselves. But total self-absorption freezes others out of their lives and often generates unkind and inconsiderate acts that build walls between people. We need to help our teenagers see that being whole and healthy involves thinking of others as well. We should teach them that in order to develop the kind of intimate and enduring relationships they want, at least occasionally, they have to be willing to put the needs of others above their own.

The Pillar of Caring connects us to others in positive ways that make relationships more rewarding and less stressful. It reminds us of the importance of being kind, considerate, and compassionate. Caring for others is not only good for those we care about; it is also good for us. When we are selfish, we may think we are looking out for ourselves, but in the long run, selfishness locks us up in a lonely dungeon.

In *The Book of Virtues* (Simon & Schuster, 1993), William Bennett describes compassion as "an active disposition toward fellowship, sharing, and supportive companionship in distress or in woe that takes very seriously the reality of other persons, their inner lives, their emotions, as well as their external circumstances." It is a virtue, he adds, that "comes close to the very heart of moral awareness, to seeing one's neighbor as another self." Jean-Jacques Rousseau agreed. He refers to compassion as a "natural feeling... that hurries us without reflection to the relief of those who are in distress."

The best way to *teach* caring, of course, is to *be* caring. In our families, one way to show we care is to spend time together, to share experiences and make real efforts to understand and appreciate each other. Parents need to spend time getting to know their children, what makes them tick, what excites them, what frightens them, what they worry about. And children should struggle to let parents in. They should also try to understand their parents. The kind of understanding that comes from caring promotes love and affection, gratitude and forgiveness, and increases our joy in one another's accomplishments. It also helps us anticipate and deal with problems before they become crises.

Being together in a caring way involves tuning in to one another, really listening, and asking questions so that we are truly a part of each other's lives.

When we talk to our teenagers about caring, we can talk about many elements of being a caring person: the ability to understand what others are feeling and experiencing, a willingness to lend a hand to help out another, and the ultimate expression of belonging – love.

Part of that discussion involves a topic near and dear to the hearts of teenagers – relationships. Talk to your teenagers about how important relationships are, but let them know that they don't have to be in a hurry to jump into a relationship just because their friends are all dating.

> '**He who sows courtesy reaps friendship, and he who plants kindness gathers love.'**
>
> – SAINT BASIL

Also talk to them about the importance of respecting others in relationships and the importance of being respected and having self-respect.

The following quotation by Margaret Anderson may help you explain different kinds of love to your teenagers: "In real love, you want the other person's good. In romantic love, you want the other person."

In the next section, we'll discuss in more detail how you can teach your teenager to be caring.

Teaching Caring

First, teach your teen what caring means. Caring and the virtues it represents – compassion, kindness, benevolence, altruism, charity, generosity, and sharing – are the heart of ethics. To be genuinely concerned with the well being of other people is an essential quality of a person of character. Teach your teen that people of character care about others. They think about how others feel, and they show that they care by being kind and helping people in need. Caring people are charitable in their thoughts and actions. They express gratitude to others and are willing to forgive.

> 'The best portion of a good man's life is his little, nameless, unremembered acts of kindness and of love.'
>
> – WILLIAM WORDSWORTH

Comment frequently about items in the news, movies, or personal events that reveal either good or bad examples of caring behavior. Teenagers can be taught that caring is not only concern but active compassion, a deep awareness of the suffering of another coupled with a wish to relieve it. Help your teenagers learn how to put themselves in the shoes of other people (empathy), how to be kind, and how to demonstrate caring by volunteering and giving money to worthy charities.

Encourage them to feel good about themselves when they care about others. Teach them that voluntarily giving time and possessions without any desire or expectation of anything except the hope, comfort, or a moment of happiness that it will give to another is the highest expression of human morality.

Enforcing Caring

Be absolutely clear that unkind, inconsiderate, and selfish behavior is unacceptable, and offer plenty of praise when your teen is generous and caring. Look for special opportunities to verbally reward teenagers who demonstrate caring, self-sacrificing, and charitable behavior.

Advocating Caring

Be certain your teenager knows that you want him or her to be a caring person, that kindness is better than cruelty, and that thinking about others is an important aspect of good character.

Modeling Caring

Remember that you teach values not merely by what you say but what you do. Be self-conscious about showing your teenager what caring behavior looks like. Write thank-you and condolence notes. Visit sick friends and relatives. Visibly give of your time and donate to charity and service organizations. Don't hesitate to point out what you are doing and why. Being explicit about your modeling isn't for self-aggrandizement; it is to make sure that your teenager observes and absorbs the lessons you want to teach.

Character in Action

Julia sighed as she dropped the groceries on the kitchen counter and saw the note from her son, Keenan.

"I got called in to work," he had written. "Home after 9."

Keenan's note meant nobody would be home for dinner this evening. That afternoon, Julia's husband, Fred, had phoned her at work to tell her that he had to have dinner with some clients who had arrived in town a day early for their regular business meeting.

Julia put the tomatoes, lettuce, and spaghetti fixings in the refrigerator and pulled a frozen dinner from the freezer. There was no reason to make a big meal for just one person.

As she waited for the microwave to deliver her Swiss steak dinner, she thought about how often her family was apart lately. Keenan was 16 now, busy with school activities and his job at the restaurant. Fred's business often kept him at the office late on weeknights, and Julia, a hospital social worker, regularly worked weekends.

Things had gotten so complicated that it recently took Julia and her sister three nights on the phone to organize a brunch for their father's birthday. Her sister's three teenagers were so overbooked that they regularly left one activity early to make it to the next one.

"This is ridiculous," Julia thought as she sat down at the big kitchen table alone. "Our lives are so complicated we don't even eat meals together. We should be smart enough to find some time to be together!"

Does Julia's life sound like yours? Do you find yourself making appointments to get together as a family? That's not uncommon today, especially for families with teenagers, where kids' school, extracurricular, and work schedules can complicate already overburdened family schedules. You try to find more time together, but somehow it never seems to work out, and you vow to try to find some other time to be together.

But think about it this way. You don't have that much time. Your teenagers will be gone from home soon, maybe in a year or two. You'll never be the same family you are right now. The clock's ticking, and each minute is important.

The Importance of Spending Time Together

When our children are young, we spend a great deal of time together as a family. Part of that togetherness stems from the basic fact that our kids are dependent upon us for necessities of life, such as diaper changes and meals.

But when those children grow into teenagers, our time together as a family diminishes. Our kids aren't as physically dependent upon us as they once were, and they want to spend more time with their friends. Add in jobs (parents' and kids'), after-school activities, and other commitments, and you have to start making appointments to see one another.

When things get that complicated, we have to work harder to find time to be together. But the effort is well worth it because spending time together strengthens our relationships with one another, solidifying the bonds we share. And it is those bonds that give us a safe haven in a world that is increasingly demanding and impersonal.

Spending time together improves communication and demonstrates caring. Parents have more time both to teach and to learn from their children, and kids have a chance to use parents and siblings as sounding boards for their ideas. When you spend time together as a family, logistics also seem easier, because family members have more opportunities to let others know about their upcoming schedules, making planning less haphazard.

As a parent of a teenager, you may think your son or daughter doesn't want to spend time with you, simply because the stereotype of a teenager is someone who prefers the company of his or her friends to the company of mom and dad. But that's not necessarily true of all teens, just as it's not necessarily true that teenagers don't listen to their parents.

That means that you have to get past the stereotypes and regularly approach your teenager with a straightforward *"Do you want to talk?"* Choose a neutral time, when you're not trying to resolve a conflict. And don't try to talk to your kids when you're rushed. Inevitably, they will feel like they're not as important as whatever else you have on your mind or your agenda.

For teenagers who are unresponsive, who really don't want to spend time with you, you may have to work harder. If they don't want to step into your world, make an effort to step into their world. Get to know their interests,

and ask questions about what they're interested in. Join in activities with them. Show you really care, that you're not just making a show of it. And don't be judgmental or condescending about what they're interested in. In addition, don't crowd them.

> **'With a sweet tongue of kindness, you can drag an elephant by a hair.'**
>
> – PERSIAN PROVERB

Give them space to be in their world, as long as they're not violating your ethical or moral standards.

And remember to use praise and encouragement to make your time together truly special.

When we spend time together as a family, we also honor the Pillars by showing that we *care* for one another, that we *respect* each other enough to make time for each other, and that we feel *responsibility* and commitment to each member of the family. Here are some suggestions for showing your teens how much you care.

Listen.

Remember the old saying about God giving us two ears but only one mouth so we can listen twice as much as we speak? It's not a bad piece of advice, and it certainly is an important part of parenting a teenager.

Teenagers are developing their own viewpoints and opinions about the world and their place in it. Sometimes, their ideas are hard to swallow. Sometimes, they are naive. It is important, however, to treat them respectfully. Teens need parents and other people in their lives to be sounding boards for their ideas and to gently but firmly redirect them if they appear to be heading off course.

But many times, teenagers just need someone to listen to them, to hear what they have to say about friends, school, and life in general, and *not* offer advice. Check in with your kids frequently. Let them know you're there to listen, and then do just that.

Talk with your kids, not at them.

Ask simple, nonthreatening questions to get their take on the world. Include them in conversations. Get their opinions on everything from where the next family vacation should be to how the President is handling the latest domestic crisis.

Be tuned in.

Teenagers lead busy lives and so do their parents. But you can still be aware of what your sons and daughters are doing and how they are reacting to the world around them by tuning into:

- **What your teenagers say to you.** Listen to what they say to get information about what they're thinking and feeling. Look for connections between things they tell you at different times to track how their thinking is progressing.

- **What they don't say.** Be tuned in to the nonverbal messages your kids send. If your usually talkative teen turns silent and moody, have a talk and find out what's going on. If you know your son or daughter is facing a particular challenge, but is not talking much about it, ask what's up. If your teen does not share information easily, try to learn to read nonverbal behaviors to determine his or her emotional level. Nonverbal behaviors might include withdrawing from the family, hanging out with new friends you don't know, or a change in personality or habits.

- **What they say about others.** Listen to what your kids say about their friends or acquaintances. You may hear some things that cause you to question those friendships.

- **Who their friends are.** Be tuned in to your teenager's friends – who they are, where they live, what interests them. Talk to them. Get to know them and their families. Make your teen's friends welcome in your home when you're there. Ask yourself if you feel comfortable with these friends. If not, talk to your kids about your concerns.

- **Where your kids go and with whom.** Set up a system for having your kids check in with you when they're away from home. (You can give negative consequences if your kids fail to use it.) Also keep tabs on your kids at home. Some families won't allow kids to have television sets or computers in their rooms so parents can monitor use of both items. Another suggestion is to watch television with your teenager and use the time together to discuss issues that come up on television shows.

- **What your kids like to do.** Knowing your kids' interests is an important part of knowing who your kids are. For example, you may not know (or want to know!) everything about the music they listen to, but at least familiarize yourself with some of the artists and the kinds of music your kids like. Making an effort means getting to know your teen better, and that will build trust between the two of you.

Be available.

Stand still long enough for your teen to find you! Be available and approachable. If you closely observe people who seem to attract teens and are often surrounded by teens, you will usually discover that they are the people who have slowed down enough to be there when kids feel like talking. Imagine yourself on a spinning carousel. It takes a lot of nerve for someone to approach you. Sometimes, our schedules and demands put us on a spinning carousel. Slow down. Better yet, get off. Be available. Here are some other tips on being available:

- **Be a volunteer chauffeur.** Volunteer to drive your teen and his or her friends to ballgames, school activities, after-school activities, anywhere and everywhere! Listen! Listen! Listen without interrupting. Show sympathy or empathy for their stresses and challenges and joys. Offer advice when it's appropriate without manipulating the conversation.

> 'You cannot do a kindness too soon, for you never know how soon it will be too late.'
>
> – RALPH WALDO EMERSON

- **Be a "shadow" helper on school and extracurricular projects.** Volunteer to help out at school and with other activities, but remember to stay in the shadows. Don't interfere as your teen works on projects or even on social problems. But be nearby, watching, supporting, encouraging. Position yourself a symbolic arm's length away, ready to help if called.

- **Struggle openly with your own challenges.** Don't hide your challenges from your teen. Let him or her know that life is a series of tough decisions for adults as well as teens. Share your decision-making process. (Make sure you are modeling an ethical decision-making process!) Instead of covering up pain, frustration, and fear, acknowledge it and share mature ways for handling those emotions. Don't reverse roles and expect your teen to parent you through your challenges. But show your teen, by example, that there are effective ways to handle life's stressors.

- **Schedule family night.** No TV. No neighbors. No friends. Just family. Take a walk. Play checkers. Feed squirrels. Eat a quiet meal together. Have everyone share his or her current challenges, fears, successes. Have everyone share the week's highlights. Talk about ways you can support one another in the coming week. Make it a night when family members can relax together and talk about what's in their hearts and on their minds.

- **Loosen up!** Have a little fun. Let your teen see your lighter side. Play ball, Ping Pong, or broom hockey. Play a table game. Dance – your style or your teen's. Skate. Keep some board games and card games on hand. (Yard sales are great sources for these items!) If necessary, schedule a little time each week for fun with your teen. It's a gift to yourself!

- **Be yourself.** Don't re-live your life through your teen. Don't try to dress, talk, and think like your teen in order to be accepted by him or her. You are the adult. Kids need adults. Secretly, they want structure and boundaries. They need mature advice, not another peer. Be a parent. You don't want peers parenting your teen.

- **Take pictures.** Capture memories. Put them in albums and add notes. Include snapshots of your teen with friends, with family, with pets. Catch them in their successes and messes. Encourage your teen to take pictures for the album, too. Sit with him or her from time to time, reviewing the albums, catching up on friendships and sharing feelings about pictured experiences.

- **Teach your teen to cook.** Even if you aren't so good at it, learn together! Let your teen pick the menu, and prepare it together. Try new recipes and make it an adventure. Make the meal a celebration, no matter how it turns out. It's a great way to spend productive time together, while learning a super skill.

- **Get to know teachers.** Drop by before or after school to say hello. Volunteer to chaperone school events. Get on a school committee. Go through your teen's school yearbook with him or her occasionally. Ask about students, teachers,

and activities. When your teen mentions an incident (good or bad) at school, show real interest
by getting him or her to show you the photos of
the people involved.

■ **Get to know your teen's dates.** Sit down in
the kitchen for a serious visit with every first
date. One mom we know has an extremely effective way of talking with her three daughters'
dates. She sits with each young man in the
kitchen and says, *"I don't know you well enough
to trust you with my checkbook, but tonight I'm
trusting you with the dearest person in my life. I
hold you personally responsible for everything
that happens to her from the time she leaves my
kitchen until you return her to my kitchen at 11
p.m. I expect you to be concerned about her welfare and safety throughout the time she is with
you, and if any harm comes to her, I hold you
personally accountable to me. If there are any situations that even threaten the presence of drugs,
alcohol, or any physical or social danger, I
expect you to bring her home immediately."* She
and her daughters have learned a lot about those
young dates from that ceremony. One dad we
know uses a similar ritual with girls his son dates
for the first time. He even calls the girls' parents
to meet them, to discuss their plans for the

evening, and to get an agreement on rules regarding safety and behavior. It works. It shows that the parents care about their teens and they are a significant presence in their lives.

- **Communicate!** Use a message board or e-mail. Put notes in socks, lunch bags, or backpacks. Have a set time for phone check-in if you must be away when your teen gets home from school. Use a pager. Identify times and methods for your teen to get in touch with you at all times. Be a constant presence in your teen's life.

- **Make your home a haven for teens.** That usually means having food in the refrigerator! Keep lemonade, soft drinks, or hot chocolate on hand. Frozen pizzas work too. Throw in a batch of homemade cookies every so often. Invite your teen's friends for spaghetti or lasagna or tacos once in a while. Let parents know that your rules and practices make your home a safe haven for teens. Board games, a basketball hoop, a VCR, and food can make your home attractive to kids. Get to know your teen by getting to know his or her friends in your home.

- **Ask good questions.** Without prying, ask sincere questions that show concern for your teen's feelings and challenges. Use phrases like, *"How do you feel about...?" "How did it make you feel*

when...?" "What if...?" "Why do you think
things happened this way?" "If you could do this
again..." "What would you do if...?"; and, most
importantly, *"What can I do to help?"*

Thoughts About Caring

Here are some quotations that you can use to launch
a discussion or make a point about various aspects of
caring:

- *In nothing do men more nearly approach the
  gods than by doing good to their fellow man.*
  – CICERO

- *We live by encouragement and die without it –
  slowly, sadly, angrily.* – CELESTE HOLM

CITIZENSHIP

I will obey the law in all matters.

I will vote in all elections and perform other civic duties such as jury duty, testifying as a witness, and reporting crimes as the opportunities arise.

I will conserve energy and avoid littering or other forms of pollution.

CHAPTER 12

Citizenship

The most important political office is that of private citizen.

– Justice Louis Brandeis

Mention citizenship to a teenager and you'll probably get a bored look and maybe a stifled yawn. But talk to kids about their ideas for the world they'll inherit, and you'll find a good number of idealists ready to shape that world into a better place.

Citizenship isn't that stuffy study of arcane laws, but idealistic participation in making the world a better place. Whenever you vote, serve on a jury, pay taxes, or preserve natural resources, you are being a good citizen.

You're also being a good citizen when you volunteer at a neighborhood school or in your community, when you voice your opinion, play by the rules, and show respect for those in authority.

Citizenship is a broad concept. As a parent, your job is to make that broad concept meaningful to your teenagers, so they can find places to make contributions to the world around them. The place to start is at home and in the community where you live.

The most powerful citizenship lesson you can give is teaching teens the importance of following the rules. Suppose for a moment your teen is participating in a basketball league. Another team approaches the league and asks to join. But this new team has a demand they want the league to meet: The new team members want to play by their own rules. They claim that the league has no right to impose its rules on them or to take away their right to choose how they want to play. They also claim it is unfair for the league to limit their freedom and try to exclude them if they don't want to play by the league's rules.

> **'There can be no daily democracy without daily citizenship.'**
>
> – RALPH NADER

Now suppose the league gives in and this team begins to play games according to its own rules. What's going to happen? The games will be chaos. The players who try to keep the league's rules will be frustrated and unhappy and see that it's unfair for them to follow the rules while the new team gets away with whatever it wants. If things continue, players, and then teams, eventually will begin to drop out of the league, and then the league itself will cease to exist.

Why does this happen? Your teen will tell you that it happened because the rules were not respected.

How is it that people understand the necessity of rules when it comes to playing basketball, but tend to generally ignore them when it comes to living in a society? Instead, people demand their "rights," their "freedom," and insist that other people tolerate their choices. The results are chaos and frustration; people "dropping out" by no longer participating, and eventually the end of an ordered, lawful society.

Citizenship is defined as the duties, rights, conduct, and responsibilities of the citizen of a state. Citizenship includes contributing to the overall public good by obeying the law, participating in the democratic process, and helping to protect the environment. Applying that to teenagers, it means keeping the rules of the family and of the community in which they live.

Teaching Citizenship

There are several things teens and adults can learn to do to be good citizens in their families and communities.

Do your share.

Because our behavior affects the people around us, we need to be aware of the people around us. In our homes, playing music too loudly, not cleaning up after ourselves, staying on the phone for hours, and being noisy late at night are all examples of bad citizenship.

In the community, breaking the glass in abandoned buildings, creating graffiti, throwing trash into the streets, speeding down neighborhood streets, and other acts of vandalism are all examples of bad citizenship.

Doing our share means that we care about and pursue the common good by trying to be a good neighbor, volunteering for things which help to make the home, community, and school better, and keeping where we live as clean as we can.

Play by the rules.

It is true, as your teenager has surely pointed out many times, that some rules are arbitrary, and rules are sometimes inconvenient. But on the theory that the line has to be drawn somewhere, rules provide a reasonable standard, and one that applies to everyone.

Playing by the rules is one way to help households, schools, and communities run smoothly. Each of us gives up some personal freedom in order to achieve collective benefits of orderliness, economic stability, personal safety, and justice.

Teens need to be taught that all of us as citizens have a bigger obligation than just to ourselves.

Respect authority.

This is probably the most difficult area for teens to conform to. They are trying to establish their own identities and independence and that often causes them to rebel against authority rather than submit to it.

But those who have been given authority, whether they are police officers, government officials, or parents, serve the greater good of the community by taking on the responsibility of protecting or acting in the best interest of those they serve. That job is only made more difficult when someone shows disrespect without cause.

Teens need to be taught that unless an authority figure has proven to be untrustworthy, he or she deserves to
be respected and obeyed.

Enforcing Citizenship

*Alonso and his friends were watching a video in the
family room when Alonso's mom walked by on her way
to do a load of laundry. She heard one of the boys make
a disparaging racial remark about one of the characters
in the video.*

*In reply, Alonso said, "Come on, Jamie. It's so igno-
rant to call somebody a name like that. How can you
stand to look so stupid?" A couple of other friends sig-
naled their approval of Alonso's comment, and then
everyone went back to watching the video.*

*Later that day, Alonso's mom praised him for what he
said to Jamie, and the voice tone he used, which was
friendly but pointed. "Thanks, Mom," Alonso said.
"Jamie didn't really know what he was saying. He'd hate
for someone to say something like that about him."*

One of the most important jobs you have as a parent
is teaching your children a set of standards for how to
live their lives. Issues like treating all people with equal
respect and behaving ethically are important lessons that
every young person must learn to be a good citizen.

For adults, teaching kids about these issues can be
difficult. The topics are sensitive and deeply personal,
and sometimes there aren't clear-cut answers.

The Six Pillars of Character can give you a good starting point for teaching and reinforcing values. Trustworthiness, respect, responsibility, fairness, caring, and citizenship are qualities that are at the root of many discussions about leading a moral life.

Another good starting point is to ask yourself *"What do I stand for?"* and *"What won't I stand for?"* for each of the foundational lessons you want to teach your kids. Once you explore your own views, it will be easier to start thinking about how you want to talk to your teenager about these issues.

Next comes the teaching. Choose a neutral time, when both you and your teenager have time and are open to the teaching. Don't try to teach when either of you is angry or distracted by other issues. You also may try teaching during one of those "teachable moments" we talked about earlier, when an issue arises in everyday conversation or events.

Start by asking your teen questions to determine what he or she knows already about the issue. Your questions also will help you find out if he or she already has an opinion about what's right. Be careful not to stop and correct your teenagers or let them know how you feel about what they are thinking while they are explaining what they know.

Then, clearly explain your take on the issue, using simple language that your teenager can understand. Give examples from your experience to show your teen why you feel the way you do. Be ready to answer questions.

Remember that your teen's questions don't necessarily mean that he or she disagrees with you. It just means he or she needs more information.

If your teenager expresses disagreement with your viewpoint, ask him or her why he or she disagrees, then calmly discuss the issue. If you believe your teen's viewpoint may place him or her in danger or violate laws, talk to him or her about your concerns. Let your teenager know that you won't negotiate on the issue, and that if he or she violates the standard you set, a consequence will follow.

The world of a teenager changes rapidly, so keep yourself open to discussions about important issues. Let your teenager know that although you have established standards, you always have time to talk. Then make the time. Remember, you don't get a second shot at parenting your teen.

Advocating Citizenship

Let your teen know how you feel about each person in the family or the community being a good citizen and looking out for the common good of everyone. Look for opportunities to both commend good citizenship and to point out the effects of bad citizenship.

Modeling Citizenship

Abe was frustrated. He and his teenage son, Jamell, had gotten a late start on their fishing trip because Jamell misplaced his tackle box and Abe had to stop for gas. So here they were, negotiating their way through morning rush-hour traffic on the interstate, when they should have been two hours away, within minutes of Lake Stuart and fishing heaven.

Traffic was picking up speed around the Benton Curve at the edge of town when a teenage boy in a fire-engine red Jeep merged wildly into a tiny space in front of Abe's aging pickup. All Abe saw was a flash of red as the Jeep roared into his lane. Abe thought his truck and the Jeep were going to bounce off each other, but the teenager accelerated, dangerously maneuvering the Jeep past the pickup.

"Damn!" Abe said, his heart racing from the near miss. Abe hit the gas to catch up with the boy. As the pickup pulled alongside the Jeep, Abe barked at Jamell: "Roll down your window!"

Jamell quickly obeyed, not wanting to aggravate his father any further.

"Hey sonny boy!" yelled Abe as he laid on the horn. "You learn how to drive or get the hell off the road. You're gonna kill somebody!" With that, Abe shook his fist at the teenager, then roared past the Jeep.

"Kids got no sense," Abe muttered to himself as Jamell sat quietly, trying to force himself to concentrate on the scenery as the truck sped down the highway.

Abe's temper got the best of him when the teenager nearly hit him on the interstate. In his anger at the care-

less driver, Abe didn't stop and think about the message
he was sending his son when he chased the other driver
and yelled at him. Abe wasn't a
very good citizen and he wasn't a
very good role model for his son.

Sometimes, we forget how
powerful an influence we have on
our kids. Even though our
teenagers supposedly distance
themselves from parental influ-
ence at every opportunity, they still look to us to be role
models for how to be good citizens.

> **'If we do not lay
> out ourselves in
> the service of
> mankind whom
> should we serve?'**
>
> – JOHN ADAMS

Many of the lessons they learn from us aren't formal
lessons at all. They pick up on what we say and do in
everyday situations, like driving in traffic. Or they watch
how we treat wait staff in a restaurant, and whether we
obey speed limits. They watch to see whether we litter, or
how we handle a complaint with a teacher. In short, our
kids learn their first lessons in Citizenship 101 from us:
how to treat other people, whether we obey laws and
rules, and how we contribute to our neighborhoods and
communities.

Our kids don't buy the old adage, "Do what I say, not
what I do." Teenagers have excellent hypocrisy radar.
They respect people who shoot straight, who are what
they seem to be. Take a look at your behavior as if you
were seeing it through your teenager's eyes. Are you a
good role model?

One way to test your role model behavior is to ask yourself how consistent you are. Consistency translates to stability for kids. And stability is an important quality in a role model. Do you follow through on promises you make? Do you show up on time when you say you'll be somewhere? Do you give a consequence when your son or daughter has earned one?

> 'Service to others is the rent you pay for your room here on earth.'
>
> – Muhammad Ali

It's also important to talk to your kids about the decisions you make, so they can see your rationales and belief system at work. A significant part of modeling is letting your kids see what drives your behavior, so they can begin to develop some rationales and belief systems of their own.

Suppose Abe had reacted differently when the other motorist cut him off. He could have provided his son a good life lesson, such as the following:

"Wow, that guy almost hit us! He must be late for the breakfast where they're giving him the good driving award, huh?" Abe said. Jamell laughed.

Abe chuckled a bit, too. "You know, I used to get really bent out of shape when somebody did something like that, but one day I just decided that I was wasting a lot of energy getting mad. I decided I didn't want to let other people's problems become my problems, you know what I mean?" Jamell nodded. It made sense to him.

In this scenario, the father showed his son a self-control strategy – using humor – that worked successfully for him. Other strategies would work equally well for other parents.

You also can teach your kids to use the Pillars or other belief systems your family holds as a mirror for their behaviors. Talk to them about the fact that even though they are not yet adults, they are still role models, for younger siblings and friends or other people in the community who may want to condemn them as lazy or destructive just because they're teenagers.

Character in Action

Peter was furious! He'd just discovered that someone had slashed all the tires on his car.

"I know Patrick and his boys did this!" he screamed. "I'm going to kick his ass right now!"

"Whoa, Peter. Settle down. Let's talk this out," his father said.

"Hell no, Dad! Did you see what they did? Those tires cost a fortune!" the teenager bellowed angrily.

The father tried to get Peter calmed down. "I know you're mad, son, but going over and beating someone up won't do any good!"

"It sure will, Dad. It'll make me feel damn good," Peter snarled. His eyes flashed in anger as he made a fist with one hand and smashed it repeatedly into the palm of his other hand. He moved toward the door to leave the house.

"Peter, come back here! You don't want to do something you'll regret!" his father said.

"NO!" Peter was walking fast now.

"Peter, you're screaming and yelling. Sit down here on the couch with me for just a minute and try to settle down so you can focus on what you need to do," Peter's father said.

The teenager stared at his dad for a few moments. Then he moved to the couch and plopped down wearily. His father sat down in the recliner next to the couch. They sat in silence for a few minutes, then went outside to look at the tires.

An hour or so later, Peter's father convinced his son to let him call the police and file a report on the tire-slashing. That evening, Peter's father talked to him about trying to control his temper and not taking the law into his own hands. Peter was still mad about the tires, but he was glad he hadn't tried to beat up Patrick. He knew his dad was right when he said, "Beating him up won't fix your tires, Peter. It'll just give you a criminal record."

The police never were able to find out who slashed the tires on Peter's car.

Peter's father used the Girls and Boys Town teaching method called *Teaching Self-Control* to help his son learn a hard lesson about revenge and citizenship. First, he helped Peter calm down by describing his problem behavior *("You're screaming and yelling.")*.

Next, the father asked Peter to sit on the couch and calm down. The father then gave Peter some quiet time to focus on regaining self-control. Later, the father did follow-up teaching aimed at giving Peter some perspective on the situation and realizing that revenge only makes matters worse.

Thoughts About Citizenship

Here are some quotations you can use to launch a discussion or make a point about various aspects of citizenship:

- *The first requisite of a good citizen in this republic of ours is that he shall be able and willing to pull his weight.* – THEODORE ROOSEVELT

- *Ask not what your country can do for you but what you can do for your country.*
  – JOHN FITZGERALD KENNEDY

CHAPTER 13

Making Effective and Ethical Decisions

Your life is the sum result of all the choices you make, both consciously and unconsciously. If you can control the process of choosing, you can take control of all aspects of your life. You can find the freedom that comes from being in charge of yourself."

– U.S. Senator Robert F. Bennett, member of a bipartisan CHARACTER COUNTS! Working Group in the Senate

Every day our teenagers make dozens of choices that affect their lives and the lives of others. Some of those choices concern schoolwork, jobs, relationships, religion, drugs, and sex. Other choices involve how they drive, whether or not they control their tempers, or whether they lie. Parents and other concerned adults can help teens make better choices.

Young people often feel a sense of powerlessness from both outside controls and inner emotions. Most teens struggle to deal with new emotions and impulses

191

that are intensified by hormonal and other physical changes. Feelings of joy and depression, anger, fear, frustration, grief, anxiety, resentment, jealousy, guilt, loneliness, love, and lust seem to come and go on their own, creating moods that may seem beyond control.

In addition, the intensity of the feelings and lack of experience make teens more apt to indulge, rather than deny, their desires and appetites. Consequently, they often act and react impulsively as if they had no choice.

We should teach teens that they may not have the power to do everything they want to do, but they still have the power to decide what to do with what they have. And that is enough power.

Power and Responsibility

First, and foremost, young people must be taught that whether or not they realize it at the time, all their words and actions, even their attitudes, reflect choices. A foundation of good decision-making is acceptance of two core principles: 1) we all have the *power* to decide what we say and how we say it, and 2) we are morally *responsible* for the consequences of our choices.

> 'We must exchange the philosophy of excuse – what I am is beyond my control – for the philosophy of responsibility.'
>
> – BARBARA JORDAN

Sometimes the power to choose is not obvious to a teenager. Young people are noto-

192

rious for laying the blame for their actions on others: *"You made me lie," "I had no choice,"* or *"It just happened."* We need to teach our children that even though they may not like the alternatives, they still have choices and the responsibility to make them wisely and ethically. What is more, the power and responsibility associated with choice exists even when it is extremely difficult to be reflective. Anger, frustration, fear, and passion are not acceptable excuses for bad choices.

Consequences and Stakeholders

Second, teens must learn to think of all their choices in terms of potential consequences that affect them and others. An important tool is a concept called "stakeholders." The idea is that each person affected by a decision has a stake in the decision and a moral claim on the decision-maker. Thus, good decisions take into account the possible consequences of words and actions on all stakeholders.

Being "thoughtful" or "considerate" about the way our choices affect others is one aspect of using the stakeholder concept. Another is to be analytical enough to be systematic and disciplined in thinking about who could be affected by a decision.

For example, suppose Charlie, a high school senior and member of the football team, is being pressured by friends to take part in a major prank involving putting glue in the door locks of classrooms. He might be less likely to participate if he thinks about all the likely consequences. Sure, preventing entry to the school may seem funny at first, but it is likely to cost a great deal of money to fix or replace the locks and the prank will disrupt the lives and plans of hundreds of teachers and students. In addition, if Charlie is caught, it's likely that he will be disciplined. If he isn't allowed to play in the next football game, his teammates and school supporters can be hurt. If he is suspended, he may not be able to attend the senior prom and his date will be greatly disappointed. His parents could be embarrassed by his choice, and the school may receive negative publicity that affects the reputation of all students if the media publicizes the story. Finally, there are the personal costs of the prank – it may affect Charlie's graduation, his chances of getting into a college, the possibility of getting or keeping an athletic scholarship, and whether he will need to go to summer school if he is suspended. If Charlie thinks about all these things before he chooses, he is more likely to make a good decision.

If teenagers can be taught to consider the likely impact of their actions and words – including physical and emotional harm to others – they are likely to make better choices and have better relationships.

But intelligent decision-making has more far-reaching effects than avoiding immediate harm to self and others. Bad choices lead to unhappy, unfulfilled lives; good choices lead to greater happiness and satisfaction in everything one does.

Making Good Choices

If we can teach children to make more effective and ethical choices, we can improve their lives and the lives of those around them. So, let's look at the components of good choices more closely.

Taking Choices Seriously

As we've said, we all make dozens, maybe hundreds, of decisions daily. The truth is that most of them do not require or justify extended forethought. They are simple and repetitive, or the outcomes are inconsequential. In such cases, it may be safe to just go with our feelings. So, it is okay to spontaneously decide what to wear and eat and what to say in casual conversations. When the issues are not morally complex and the stakes are not high, our normal instincts are sufficient.

Unfortunately, teenagers often do not distinguish between these sorts of minor issues and those where the potential consequences can be substantially higher. As a result, they have a tendency to do what they feel like doing – "go with the flow" – in situations that merit a much more careful approach.

Think of the choices that our children regularly face: study or not study for a test; cut school with a friend or go to class; make fun of, tease, or bully a classmate or defend a classmate who is being picked on; experiment with drugs or say "No"; drink a beer or abstain from using alcohol; lie to a teacher or tell the truth; borrow a friend's property without asking or ask for permission;

talk back to a parent or accept what the parent says; report a threat made by a fellow student or keep it secret. While many of these decisions may not seem important at first glance, all have potentially momentous consequences.

Recognizing Important Decisions

Since reflection does not come naturally to teens, parents should, from the earliest age, sharpen their children's instincts about what is important and what is not.

At the very least, we can give our children guidance that will help them recognize when reflection and caution are most needed. The simple formula is: the greater the potential consequences, the more need there is for careful decision-making. Thus, choices that can cause serious physical or emotional harm are high-stakes decisions. So are those that can harm a reputation or create major barriers to the achievement of long-term personal goals. If you can teach your teen to ask these four questions, he or she will be better able to identify important decisions:

1. Is there possible danger of physical harm to me or anyone else?

2. Could I or someone else suffer serious emotional pain?

3. Could the decision hurt my reputation, undermine my credibility, or damage important relationships?

4. Could the decision impede the achievement of any important goal?

Making Effective and Ethical Decisions

Good decisions are both *effective* and *ethical*.

Effective Decisions

A decision is effective if it accomplishes something we *want* to happen, if it advances our purposes, goals, or objectives. A simple test is: Are you satisfied with the results? A choice that produces unintended and undesirable results is ineffective.

For example, if we make a casual remark to make someone feel good but it makes him or her feel bad instead, we were ineffective. Similarly, if a teen decided to do something she really didn't want to do just to please a friend, and the decision ended up getting her in serious trouble, it's a bad decision.

The key to making effective decisions is to think about choices in terms of their ability to accomplish our most important goals. This means we have to understand the difference between immediate and short-term goals, and longer-range goals.

Example: Derek and Cheating. Derek is facing an important test and he needs a good grade in order to play in a weekend soccer game. His immediate goal is to get a good grade to accomplish another goal: to play in the game. Cheating on the test may be an effective way to accomplish this. But what if he is caught? Not only will he not get a good grade and not be able to play in the game, much more serious results may occur. He may flunk the class and have to go to summer school, be suspended from school, or be expelled from the team. Any of these consequences would surely defeat other more important objectives. And even if Derek is not caught, his decision to cheat puts him on a path of moral compromise that is absolutely certain to negatively affect his attitudes toward honesty, his self-image, and his reputation among those who know him.

Ethical Decisions

A decision is ethical when it is consistent with the Six Pillars of Character – ethical decisions generate and sustain trust; demonstrate respect, responsibility, fairness, and caring; and are consistent with our obligations of good citizenship. If we lie to get something we want and we get it, the decision can be called effective but it is also unethical.

> 'When your values are clear to you, making decisions becomes easier.'
>
> – Roy Disney

If we are going to teach the ethical aspect of good decision-making, it will be helpful to understand better how we distinguish good decisions from bad decisions and what processes tend to yield better choices. Let's start with recognizing that there are two critical aspects to ethically sound decisions: knowing what to do and doing it.

Discernment. The first requirement of good decisions is *discernment,* the ability to know the difference between right and wrong, between ethical and unethical behavior. This involves true understanding of the core ethical values discussed in previous chapters. It is not obvious to some children, for example, that it is just as dishonest (and unethical) to deliberately deceive someone by half-truths and trickery as it is to tell an outright lie. And if a youngster confuses the ethical obligation to treat everyone with respect with the idea of actually holding a person in high esteem, he or she may not properly distinguish between acceptable and unacceptable behavior. Discernment requires knowledge and judgment.

Discipline. Good decisions also require *discipline,* the strength of character to do what should be done even when it is costly or uncomfortable. It's not enough that we decide to do something. That choice does not become a good decision until it is translated into action. This often takes willpower or moral courage: the willingness to do the right thing even when it is inconvenient, scary, difficult, or costly.

Example: Dad and Michael. Dad is both worried and furious. His son, Michael, is more than two hours late returning from a school event. As the clock ticks away the minutes, Dad is going over in his mind all the things he can say and do to make Michael understand that his behavior is unacceptable. He reviews in his mind a hard and direct confrontation that may well involve raised voices and heated tempers. This type of setting is the breeding ground for bad decisions.

If Dad wants to make an effective and ethical decision and avoid doing something foolish and impulsive, he must set aside his emotions long enough to allow him to think clearly about his objectives, both short term and long term. His most immediate desire may be to vent his anger and frustration in the belief that it will teach his son a lesson. Yet his longer-term goal is to help his son become more responsible and respectful. And he would surely like to strengthen rather than weaken his relationship with Michael and the quality of their communications.

If Dad thinks about these potentially conflicting goals, he should realize how important it is to choose his words and his tone carefully. His decision on how to handle this situation is an important one that could significantly affect his relationship with his son, and perhaps, his son's character.

Dad must decide whether his most important goal is to let off steam and say what's on his mind, regardless of the consequences, or to turn this situation into a positive teaching moment.

Is Dad more concerned about being sure Michael knows how angry he is, or is he more interested in trying to get Michael to think and act differently in the future? Does Dad want a forced apology or real remorse? Does he want to make Michael feel bad or angry? How important is it that he show that he is in control as opposed to developing a more respectful, mature relationship with his son? Obviously, the answer to these questions would greatly affect the way Dad reacts.

If we fail to adequately consider our choices in terms of the longer-term consequences, we often accomplish short-term objectives (fully expressing anger) at the cost of our long-term goals. Thus, Dad must realize that both the tone and content of his reaction will either advance or undermine his more important objectives regarding Michael.

Good decisions help us achieve our major goals, poor ones impede us from doing so. In this setting, it would seem clear that it would help Dad to calm down and adopt a strategy to have a meaningful discussion rather than an explosive confrontation. Yet controlling our emotions to that extent takes enormous moral willpower.

This is a good example where both discernment and discipline play crucial roles. All the questions discussed earlier are part of a reflective process that should help Dad realize that he should be sure that his reactions don't injure his relationship with his son. He knows he should control his temper and develop a thoughtful strategy. But knowing and doing are two different things.

It will take a tremendous amount of discipline for Dad to overcome his anger. Yet isn't that precisely what we want our children to do? If Dad handles the situation effectively, he will model good decision-making and increase the likelihood that Michael will learn to do likewise.

It's also a good example showing the interrelationship of effectiveness and ethics. The reason an impulsive angry reaction is likely to undermine Dad's relationship goals is that the most likely consequences of such behavior will be a defensive and equally angry reaction from Michael.

And keep in mind, at this stage, Dad doesn't even know why Michael is late. Perhaps there are good and persuasive reasons (e.g., he had to take a friend to the hospital or his car broke down). In any event, to react without first giving his son an opportunity to explain is unfair.

In addition, if Dad yells at his son, no matter how justified Dad thinks he is, Michael will feel abused and disrespected. Would Dad yell at an employee who was equally late? Sometimes, parents forget that their children have as much right to be treated with dignity as strangers.

Example: Cindy and Her Mom. Cindy, a tenth-grade girl, really wants to go to a party being held by seniors. She's sure there will be drinking but if her mom knows that, she will be forbidden from going. In fact, her mom would never let her go to a party unless she knew the parents of the host. Her friend, Jackie, suggests that Cindy lie to her mom and say she is going to study with Jackie and spend the night. Jackie says her mom is cool and would back them up if she had to. Should Cindy do it?

Cindy's immediate goal is clear: She wants to go to the party. But if she would stop and think about the potential consequences of a decision to lie to her mom, she would also realize that the choice might become a serious obstacle to other things she wants even more, such as her mother's trust, greater personal freedom, and avoiding punishment that could result if she is caught.

She also has to realize that even if the decision was effective in getting her to the party, and even if she gets away with her lie, her choice is not an ethical one. It's wrong to lie, especially to someone who trusts you, whether or not the person finds out. We must teach our teens that *our character is revealed by how we act when we think we will never be found out.*

Of course, when decisions are made that affect important personal relationships, issues of effectiveness and ethics are entwined. Thus, Cindy must be taught to recognize this as a very important decision that could have dramatic and long-term consequences on her life. Even though she is likely to minimize the risks in her mind because she is sure she won't get caught, Cindy should understand that she might accomplish the short-term goal of going to the party at the cost of a long-term

> **'Character may be manifested in the great moments, but it is made in the small ones.'**
>
> – PHILLIPS BROOKS

desire to build and maintain a healthy and trusting relationship with her mother.

Many poor decisions follow this pattern; they achieve short-term goals at a very heavy price that a thoughtful person would not pay.

A Decision-Making Process

Parents can teach and model good decision-making by teaching this seven-step process:

1. Stop and Think

One of the most important and effective steps in making better decisions is the oldest advice in the world: Think ahead. To do this, it's necessary to first stop the momentum of events long enough to permit calm analysis. This often requires substantial discipline, but it can be a powerful antidote to the causes of poor choices.

The well-worn formula to count to ten when angry and to one hundred when very angry is a simple technique designed to prevent foolish and impulsive behavior. But just as we are more apt to make foolish decisions when we are angry, we also are under the influence of powerful desires and passions or fatigue when we are in a hurry or under pressure and when we are ignorant of important facts.

We need to train youngsters to stop long enough to prevent thoughtless behavior with a forced moment of reflection. Just like we teach our children to look both ways before they cross the street, we can and should instill the habit of looking ahead when considering other decisions.

Stopping to think provides two benefits. First, it helps discernment by increasing the likelihood that we will do a better job of sorting out facts and alternatives and choosing the most effective and ethical course of action. Second, it can allow us to mobilize the discipline – the moral willpower – to do what we know we should.

2. Clarify Goals

Before choosing, we must clarify in our own mind what we want to accomplish both now and in the future. Determine which of those goals is the most important. Remember that decisions that satisfy immediate wants and needs often can prevent a person from achieving more important long-term goals.

3. Determine Facts

Once we have a clear picture of the short-term and long-term goals that may be affected by a decision, we must be sure we have adequate information to support an intelligent choice. We can't make good decisions if we don't know the facts.

To determine the facts, first resolve what you know and what you need to know. Be prepared to get additional information and to verify assumptions and other uncertain forms of information.

Next, determine if the information you have is complete and reliable, so that you can make a reasoned judgment as to the facts and possibilities.

Once we begin to be more careful about gathering facts, we find that there can be disagreements or different versions of the facts. In these situations, part of making good decisions involves making good judgments as to who and what to believe. Here are some guidelines for making those judgments:

- **Consider the reliability and credibility of the people who are giving you facts.** In general, you can trust most information from the people you trust most.

- **Consider the basis of the supposed facts.** If the person giving you the information says he or she personally heard or saw something, evaluate whether you consider that person trustworthy in terms of honesty, accuracy, and memory.

- **Remember that assumptions, gossip, and hearsay are not the same as facts.**

- **Consider all perspectives** but be careful to consider whether the source of the information has values that are different from yours or has a bias or self-interest that could affect the source's perception of the facts.

- **Where possible, seek out the opinions of people whose judgment and character you**

respect. But be careful to distinguish between well-grounded opinions from well-informed people and casual speculation, conjecture, and guesswork.

4. Develop Options

Now that you know what you want to accomplish and you've made your best judgment as to the relevant facts, make a mental or written list of options, a range of things you could do to accomplish your goals.

If you're facing an especially important decision, find someone you trust to talk to so that you can broaden your perspective and think of new choices. If you can think of only one choice, you're not thinking hard enough.

5. Consider Consequences

Two techniques help reveal the potential consequences:

■ **"Pillar-size" your options.** We use this term for the sake of simplicity to describe a process of filtering your choices through each of the Six Pillars of Character: trustworthiness, respect, responsibility, fairness, caring, and citizenship. Will the action you are considering violate any of the core ethical principles? (Does it involve lying or breaking a promise? Is it disrespectful to anyone? Is it irresponsible, unfair, or uncaring? Does it involve breaking laws or rules?) Eliminate illegal and unethical options.

- **Identify the stakeholders and how the decision is likely to affect them.** Consider your choices from the point of view of the major stakeholders. Identify who will be helped and who might be hurt by the decision.

6. Choose

Once you've clarified your goals, determined the facts, developed options, and considered the consequences of each option, it is time to choose. If it is not immediately clear what decision you should make, see if any of the following strategies help:

- **Talk to someone whose judgment you respect.** Whenever you can, get the perspective of someone whose judgment you respect. Although a friend or contemporary is more likely to understand and identify with your emotions, a caring adult is likely to have more experience and a wider perspective that can be very helpful. Once you've gathered opinions and advice, consider them with an open mind, but remember the ultimate responsibility for the choice is yours.

- **Ask yourself: What would the most ethical person I know do?** Think of the person (in real life or fiction) you know or know of who has the strongest character and best ethical judgment. Then ask yourself: What would that person do in this situation? Think of that person as your decision-making role model and try to behave the way he or she would behave.

Many Christians wear a small bracelet with the letters WWJD; the letters stand for "What would Jesus do?" Whether you are Christian or not, however, the idea of referencing a higher spiritual or moral force is a useful one. You could translate the question into: "What would God want me to do?" "What would Buddha or Allah do?" "What would the Dalai Llama do?" "What would the most virtuous person in the world do?"

- **What would you do if you were sure everyone would know about your decision?** If everyone you know would find out about your decision, would you be proud and comfortable? Choices that look good only if no one knows about them are always bad choices. Good choices make us worthy of admiration and build good reputations. It's been said that character is *revealed* by how we behave when we think no one is looking, but character is *strengthened* when we act as if everyone is looking.

- **Follow the Golden Rule: Do unto others as you would have them do unto you.** The Golden Rule is one of the oldest and best guides to ethical decision-making. If we treat people the way we want to be treated, we are likely to live up to the Six Pillars of Character. We don't want to be lied to or have promises broken, so we should be honest and keep our promises to others. We want others to treat us with respect, so we should treat others respectfully.

7. Monitor and Modify

Since most decisions are based on imperfect information and "best effort" predictions, it is inevitable that some of them will be wrong. Even the most carefully considered decisions don't always come out the way we expected or wanted. Ethical decision-makers monitor the effects of their choices. If they are ineffective because they are not producing the intended results or are causing additional unintended and undesirable results, ethical decision-makers will assess the situation and make new decisions based on current information.

Real-Life Situations

The real-life situations in this section may provide some talking points for you and your teenager – an opportunity to discuss how to make better choices. The situations presented here are rooted in common situa-

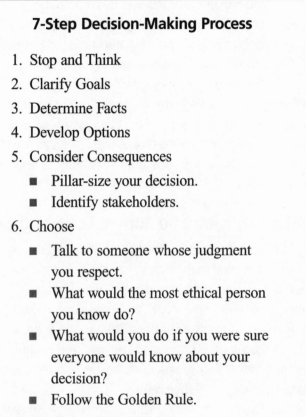

7-Step Decision-Making Process

1. Stop and Think
2. Clarify Goals
3. Determine Facts
4. Develop Options
5. Consider Consequences
   - Pillar-size your decision.
   - Identify stakeholders.
6. Choose
   - Talk to someone whose judgment you respect.
   - What would the most ethical person you know do?
   - What would you do if you were sure everyone would know about your decision?
   - Follow the Golden Rule.
7. Monitor and Modify

tions teenagers experience. We encourage you to read the stories with your teenager, then talk about them, the ethical questions they raise, and the Pillars involved. The situations provide a good forum for discussions about how to sort through situations when our heads and our hearts don't agree.

As you engage your teens in discussion, be sure to do your best to find out what they value and how they think about problems. Ask probing questions to get them to think through the situations and figure out where they stand. Question them about their choices. Let them know where you stand, and why. Believe it or not, studies show that teens do care what their parents think, especially when those parents have shown their teenagers that they value their teens' opinions and their ability to make good ethical choices.

Situation: Jan and Tony – Love and Sex

Jan is a junior in high school. She has dated Tony for six months, and she is pretty sure she is in love with him. Jan is a serious student and hasn't dated much. Tony is a freshman at the junior college in the same town. Tony is a good-looking guy, but doesn't know what he wants to do in the future. His parents are paying his tuition and helping with living expenses, so he only has to work part-time doing telemarketing.

Jan and Tony see each other every Friday and Saturday night. Tony doesn't have much money so they often go to his apartment and fix a meal or watch movies. Sometimes they go for a walk or sit out on the steps and talk for hours. Jan doesn't tell her parents this, however, because they wouldn't like the two of them being alone at his apartment. Jan's girlfriends think Tony is very cool, and they think Jan is lucky to have an older boyfriend who has his own place.

Lately, Jan has become concerned about their relationship. It seems like Tony isn't interested in doing much. He doesn't want to talk and laugh as much as he did before. He says he's tired and just wants to kick back and relax. Usually, Tony just wants to sit and watch TV. That always leads to make-out sessions. Jan doesn't really mind, but lately he has been pressuring her to go further than kissing.

Jan feels confused. She thinks she loves Tony and Tony says he loves her, but she has always wanted to wait until she got married to have sex. She just feels like that's the right thing to do. She feels she would lose respect for herself if she went against what she believed. Jan also worries about being used, getting pregnant, and getting a sexually transmitted disease. Jan also knows that her parents would be very disappointed in her, and although they might not find out, it still eats at her conscience.

Jan decides to talk to her best friend Melissa about the problem: Should she have sexual intercourse with Tony? After hearing Jan's concerns, Melissa tells Jan that she is probably the only junior girl who hasn't had sex and that she is making too much of it. "Go for it, girl, or you're going to lose Tony!" Melissa says.

What should Jan do?

Probing Values and Beliefs

Jan and Tony obviously care about each other. They may even be in love. Here are some general questions to consider:

- Is loving someone enough of a reason to have sex?

- If Tony loves Jan, is it right for him to pressure her to have sex? Why or why not?

- If Jan loves Tony, is it right for her to refuse to have sex? Why or why not?

- When two people care about or love each other very much, should there ever be any limits or rules to what each person expects of the other? If so, what should those limits and rules be? How do such limits tie into the character Pillars we've discussed?

- Should Jan be expected to sacrifice her self-respect in order to save her relationship with Tony? Why or why not?

- How do you think Tony views this situation?

- What might happen if Jan gives in to Tony? What might happen if she doesn't?

- If Jan was your daughter, and came to you with this problem, what would you say or do?

At first, the number of questions you ask to analyze the situation may seem overwhelming, but as you practice, the habits of thinking become more intuitive and rapid. Now let's apply a more rigorous decision-making process.

Decision-Making Process

1. **Stop and think.** This is certainly a decision that should be made thoughtfully and not in a moment of pressure or passion. Jan must be sure that she thinks this through.

2. **Clarify goals.** Let's look at the problem in the context of Jan's goals. Remember, a good decision is both effective and ethical. Therefore, Jan's decision is a good one only if it accomplishes her most important goals and is consistent with core ethical values.

- In deciding whether to have sex with Tony, what does she want to accomplish in terms of her long- and short-term relationship with Tony and her ambitions for her own life? Among the possibilities: to preserve and strengthen her relationship with Tony; to advance her relationship with Tony toward marriage; or to determine whether her relationship with Tony is healthy and is what she wants in the long run.

- She should also consider how she wants Tony and others, including her parents, to think of her.

- Finally, she might want to examine what her real goal is: keeping Tony, having a good and stable relationship with some boy, or preparing herself to have a good marriage with someone in the future.

3. Determine facts. Are there facts that Jan should know before she makes a decision? (See information on pages 218-219.) Although the impact of her decision cannot be known for certain, Jan still has to determine what outcomes she believes are most likely and what risks are acceptable. Here are some questions she should ask:

- What will Tony's short-term and long-term attitude be toward the relationship be if she sleeps with him?

- Does Tony love her enough that he would accept her decision not to sleep with him?

- How is Jan likely to feel about herself if she decides to sleep with him to preserve their relationship?

- If Jan feels she compromised her principles to save the relationship, will that cause resentment that will ultimately defeat the relationship?

- If Tony turns out not to be the one, how is the decision she will make now likely to affect future relationships with others?

- What are the practical risks of pregnancy and/or sexually transmitted diseases?

4. Develop options. Jan is likely to believe that she has only two choices: sleep and keep Tony or hold back and lose Tony. Are there other options?

Are there other ways to strengthen her relationship with Tony without sex? What about talking to Tony directly and fully?

5. Consider consequences.

■ What Pillars of Character are involved in Jan's decision? Integrity, an aspect of trustworthiness, is about being true to one's own principles. Is Tony being honest with her? In what ways is respect involved? How about responsibility, fairness, and caring?

■ Who are the stakeholders besides Jan and Tony? Consider Jan's parents, Jan's future boyfriends, and children. How about the example she is setting for her peers or siblings?

6. Choose. Jan should seek out the perspective and advice from an adult she trusts. This is a common problem that almost every woman has gone through, but responsible males can also offer important insights on the man's perspective.

If Jan decides to sleep with Tony not because it's what she wants or feels ready for but because it is the only way to keep Tony or be cool among her peers, how does the decision look from the perspective of the publicity test? Would Jan be comfortable if everyone knew that she was having sex with Tony and her true reasons for doing it? What does she think the most ethical person she knows would do in such a situation? What would her ethical role model advise?

7. **Monitor and modify.** Whatever Jan decides to do, she should be observant about the reactions and results and be willing to modify her decision to accomplish her most important goals.

Facts About Teen Sexual Activity

The following data about teen sexual activity are from the 2000 Youth Risk Behavior Surveillance survey conducted by the National Centers for Disease Control:

■ Half of all high school students had sexual intercourse, half were still virgins.

■ 42% of currently sexually active students reported that neither they nor their partner had used a condom during last sexual intercourse.

■ 84% of currently sexually active students reported that neither they nor their partner had used birth control pills during last sexual intercourse.

■ 25% of currently sexually active students had used alcohol or drugs at last sexual intercourse.

■ 13% of all high school girls reported that they had been forced to have sexual intercourse when they did not want to.

- 16% of all high school students had had sexual intercourse during their lifetime with four or more partners.

- 6% of all high school students reported that they had been pregnant or had gotten someone else pregnant.

- 12% of male high school students and 4% of females had initiated sexual intercourse before age 13.

While the rates of some sexually-transmitted diseases (STDs) like syphilis are declining among teens and other age groups, other STDs like chlamydia and herpes may be increasing, particularly in areas where there are no educational or treatment programs for teenagers, the CDC reported in its study, "Tracking the Hidden Epidemics: Trends in STDs in United States 2000." The report said teenagers and young adults are at high behavioral risk for acquiring most STDs because they are more likely than people in other age groups to have multiple sex partners, to engage in unprotected sex, and for young women, to choose sexual partners older than themselves.

Situation: Misty and Sonja – No Sale

Misty and Sonja are best friends. They were neighbors from the time they were little until they were in the eighth grade, when Sonja's parents got divorced and

Sonja and her mom moved to an apartment across town. Misty and Sonja talk on the phone daily and get together at least once every weekend. They enjoy the same things – riding bikes, talking about boys, and shopping.

One Saturday while they were shopping at a mall, Sonja took a bunch of clothes into the dressing room to try on. Misty waited for her, and they left the store together. Just outside the store Misty asked, "Why didn't you get any of the outfits you tried on?"

"I got all of them!" Sonja replied. "I got the five-finger discount. I had a big shopping bag from this store folded up in my purse. No one even noticed. And I took the one you liked for you. Here, take it."

Standing outside the store, Misty is nervous and upset. She knows it is wrong to shoplift, and she's afraid that Sonja will get caught. Misty is also afraid she will be accused of stealing because she was with Sonja, especially if she takes the outfit she is offered. She is disturbed and disappointed that her friend was willing to steal but she doesn't want to make a big deal about it. She doesn't want to ruin the friendship or make Sonja feel bad because she knows Sonja's family doesn't have much money.

But she also worries that if she doesn't try to help Sonja see what she did was wrong, it could ruin her character and reputation. Finally, she worries that if her friend continues on this path she will continually make bad choices that could mess up the rest of her life.

What should Misty do?

Conflicting Values

This problem presents questions about conflicting values. Misty values her friendship with Sonja and wants to be caring, respectful, and loyal to her, but she also has her own strong beliefs about honesty, responsibility, and citizenship and she knows that stealing is just plain wrong. Since the two girls are together, there is a real risk that if Sonja is caught Misty will be accused of helping her. Finally, there is a conflict as to what is really in the best interest of Sonja.

- Should Misty let Sonja think stealing is okay or, just as she would try to stop a friend from hurting herself or driving while drunk, should Misty try to stop Sonja?

- Would a good friend just turn the other way or try to intervene and counsel?

- If Sonja's parents had good values, what do you think they would do if they found out what Sonja was doing? Is that parental perspective appropriate or inappropriate for a caring friend?

- If Misty was your daughter, and she came to you with this problem, what would you say or do?

Let's see how the decision-making process might help sort out the issues.

Decision-Making Process

1. **Stop and think.** Misty doesn't have much time to process this decision but she needs to self-con-

sciously stop the momentum of events to think this through. If she takes the outfit or even leaves the mall with Sonja, she may have become an accomplice (a partner) to Sonja's crimes.

2. **Clarify goals.** As Misty confronts this complex problem, she needs to think about what she wants to accomplish in making the decision.

- If her only goal is to maintain a friendship with Sonja without friction, the option of saying nothing looks attractive. As we will see in a moment, however, that choice raises issues of both effectiveness and ethics.

- What if her friendship and affection for Sonja is so strong (as love is from a parent to a teen) that she is more concerned with Sonja's long-term welfare than being liked? If her goal is to do the thing most likely to help Sonja, a different set of options might be better.

- Finally, Misty can't lose sight of her own goals and objectives. If she takes the outfit that she knows is stolen and hangs around a person who shoplifts, is she likely to get involved or in trouble in ways that undermine her own personal goals for her life and reputation?

3. **Determine facts.** The facts here are clear. Sonja told her she stole the clothing. How is Sonja likely to respond if Misty states her opinion of

Sonja's actions? Or what if Misty takes an even stronger position, telling her to return the goods on threat of reporting the theft. Although it's hard to predict another's actions, and the actual reaction would depend on the tact with which the message was delivered, it's probably safe to conclude that Sonja will not be pleased and could well terminate the relationship.

On the other hand, there is also the "fact" of how Misty will feel about Sonja and the friendship if she says and does nothing. From an effectiveness point of view, it's possible that trying to preserve the relationship by saying nothing is not a realistic option because the relationship is bound to change as a result of Misty's discomfort with Sonja's actions and values.

4. **Develop options.** Misty should think of all her options, including taking the outfit and saying nothing, refusing the outfit with or without a moral lecture, trying to convince Sonja to return the goods, insisting that Sonja return the goods, or reporting Sonja to the store owner.

Even after she leaves the mall, Misty will have continuing problems and options: talking to Sonja about the whole matter, terminating her relationship with Sonja, talking to friends about the incident as gossip or to seek advice, telling

Sonja's mother, talking to her own parents or a teacher or counselor.

5. **Consider consequences.** What ethical Pillars are involved? This scenario raises quite a few serious ethical principles.

■ Most obvious are the principles of trustworthiness and citizenship. Stealing and accepting stolen property constitute serious dishonest behavior and are criminal acts. Regardless of her initial intent, if Misty takes the outfit, she has definitely committed a crime. Even if she doesn't take the outfit but she says nothing, she could be accused of being an accomplice and she still might be convicted. Even if she is not convicted, it could seriously hurt her reputation and embarrass her family.

■ The situation also raises issues of loyalty (part of trustworthiness), caring, and respect. One argument is that a loyal caring friend ought to respect Sonja's decisions and support her.

■ Better understanding of these principles, however, yields the conclusion that a truly caring and loyal friend looks out for the long-term welfare of a friend and tries to stop him or her from doing reckless and self-destructive things.

■ In addition, Sonja's conduct could be interpreted as disrespectful and disloyal to Misty. (She sub-

jects her to serious trouble without her consent
and against Misty's values and beliefs.)

■ Finally, there is the issue of responsibility.
Clearly, Misty is morally as well as legally
accountable for the choices she will make, both
with regard to the theft and the question of ignoring Sonja's serious character and behavioral flaws
or intervening in some way to modify her friend's
attitudes and actions.

Who are the major stakeholders? Besides
Misty and Sonja, the parents of both girls, the
storeowner, and the whole community have a
stake in Sonja's conduct and Misty's decision
about what to do.

6. **Choose.** This is a true ethical dilemma with no
easy answers. No matter what Misty does, it will
feel bad. Still she must choose. Doing nothing in
a situation like this is a choice. Seeking an adult
advisor is not an immediate option. She must
decide whether to leave the mall with Sonja and
whether to accept the outfit now. So she should
apply the other three tests. What would the most
ethical person she knows do? What would she do
if she knew her decision would be well publi-
cized?

Both of these strategies should lead Misty to
conclude that accepting the outfit is clearly

wrong and that even leaving the mall without saying anything is wrong.

The Golden Rule test may be the least helpful here because it depends on what "others" you think about. Sonja is not the only stakeholder here. What about the storeowner?

7. **Monitor and modify.** This is an ongoing situation with a long duration. No matter what she decides to do on the spot, Misty must deal with the aftermath and be prepared to monitor and modify her choices in the context of the results and new information.

Situation: Juan and Western Civ

It is finally the end of Juan's senior year! Juan can't wait to graduate and work full-time for the local car dealership where he has been working part-time. The dealership is even sending him to a training center for three weeks to learn about appraising auto body damage. There is just one problem that might hamper his good fortune: He has to pass the Western Civilization final. If he doesn't, he won't graduate.

Juan is going in for help from his teacher as much as he can but it is hard to find time because of his work schedule.

A few days before finals, Vince stops Juan in the hallway. "Look what I just lifted from Ms. McKay's desk drawer!" says Vince. In Vince's hand is the key to Ms.

McKay's file cabinet. "Now we don't have to worry about that Western Civ final, man! I saw her put the final in there today. It's just sitting there waiting for us."

"I don't know about this," says Juan.

"It'll be easy," Vince says. "You go in for help after school, and I'll call the office and ask to speak to Ms. McKay. I'll ask her some stupid question about the assignment that's due tomorrow so you'll have time to grab the test. Then tomorrow morning, *after* you've made copies of the test, we'll do the same routine. We'll have the keys back before she misses them."

Juan feels uneasy about the whole situation. Ms. McKay is one of his favorite teachers. But she is tough, and Juan knows the Western Civilization final will be the hardest test he's ever taken. He just has to pass that final.

What should Juan do?

Decision-Making Process

1. **Stop and think.** Juan needs to carefully consider what he will do.

2. **Clarify goals.** What should Juan be thinking about here in terms of his immediate and long-term goals? What are his most important goals that could be affected by the choice he is about to make?

3. **Determine facts.** What should Juan know to make a better decision?

4. **Develop options.** If Juan's immediate objective is to pass the test, what options does he have other than cheating? List everything Juan could realistically do.

5. **Consider consequences.** What Pillars of Character are involved in the choices Juan faces? Who are the stakeholders?

6. **Choose.** If the decision isn't obvious (and it should be in this case – don't cheat!), consider how the various decision-making strategies would guide a choice.

7. **Monitor and modify.** After Juan makes a decision, he must be prepared to monitor and modify it for effectiveness and ethics.

Situation: Kenny and the Bully

Les is known as a troublemaker and a bully in school. He never does his homework and constantly interrupts class with his unruly behavior and smart-mouth comments. He hangs around with a group of guys who share his lack of interest in school and his knack for getting into trouble. Les and his buddies don't like the "jocks" or the "study nerds" in the school, and they aren't shy about letting everyone know how they feel about those students.

Kenny is one of the study nerds that Les doesn't like. Les often threatens and picks on Kenny in class and in the halls, but Kenny just lets it slide. He knows some kids who talked back to Les, and they got beat up by Les and his friends.

One night after a mentoring group had met at the school, Kenny walks out to the parking lot and finds Les "keying" the principal's car. Kenny tries to act like he hasn't seen it, but Les walks up to him and grabs him by his shirt collar.

"If you breathe a word about what you saw, you will die!" Les whispers.

"No problem, man! I didn't see a thing," says Kenny.

A few minutes later, while Kenny is waiting at the bus stop, the principal leaves the school and notices that his car has been damaged. He walks over to the bus stop and says, "Kenny, I trust you. Did you see who did this to my car?"

Kenny is afraid of Les and scared that he might be accused of doing the damage. What should Kenny do? What should Kenny do if the principal mistakenly blames another student for the vandalism? If you were Les's parent, how would you go about changing his behavior, especially the way he treats others?

Decision-Making Process

1. **Stop and think.** Kenny needs to take some time to consider the situation and his role in it.

2. **Clarify goals.** What should Kenny be thinking about here in terms of his immediate and long-

term goals? What are the most important goals that could be affected by the choice he is about to make?

3. **Determine facts.** What should Kenny know to make a better decision?

4. **Determine options.** If Kenny's immediate objective is to avoid being beaten up, what options does he have other than lying to the principal? List everything Kenny could realistically do.

5. **Consider consequences.** What Pillars of Character are involved in the choices Kenny faces? Who are the stakeholders?

6. **Choose.** Consider how the various decision-making strategies would guide a choice.

7. **Monitor and modify.** After he makes a decision, Kenny must realize that he still must monitor the situation and adjust his actions.

Some Final Thoughts

In a world that worships teenage superstars and quick-fix success, it may seem an act of extreme faith to teach your kids about character. Why would anyone care about trustworthiness when it's more important to have cool friends and a sports car? Or why would you talk about responsibility when it's easier to let whatever's going to happen just happen?

The answer may be that the only tool we can give our kids to navigate in such a world is strong character. With it, our kids have a compass to find a meaningful life. Without it, they have little else that matters.

Father Flanagan made sure that character lessons were an integral part of life at his home for boys, the place that today is Girls and Boys Town. He once told a group of youth, "You have learned during your stay here the proper principles on which a real and successful life is founded. You have built characters on love and service. As long as you keep before your mind these great and eternal truths, you shall not fail."

> **'Character, not circumstances, makes the man.'**
>
> – BOOKER T. WASHINGTON

We hope you've found some lessons worth teaching in this book and some ideas about using head, heart, and habits to make the world a more ethical and moral place. We hope you'll use the Six Pillars of Character and the Girls and Boys Town teaching methods to help your kids become good people who care about doing what's right.

In addition, we hope you'll take a moment and congratulate yourself for your continuing commitment to rearing a teenager who can and will make a difference in the world. That is indeed an awesome legacy.

Index

Credits

Editing:	Elizabeth Gauger
	Terry Hyland
Design and Layout:	Anne Hughes
Production:	Mary Steiner

009-19-0043